That Sum

'Learning that David Edgar was tackling the 1984 miners' strike you would probably know what to expect – a big play, now in Orgreave, now Westminster, now the NUM HQ; now shields, public meetings, crowd scenes, and two page speeches.

You would be surprised. *That Summer* – Edgar's elegantly tangential treatment of the dispute – is an exquisite little play, an odd but almost wholly successful marriage of the political drama with the domestic comedy.' Mark Lawson, *Plays and Players*.

That Summer was premiered at the Hampstead Theatre, London, in July 1987. It was directed by Michael Attenborough.

DAVID EDGAR was born in 1948 in Birmingham. His stage work – some forty plays in all – includes *Excuses Excuses* (1972); *Dick Deterred* (1974); *Saigon Rose* (1976); *Wreckers* (1977); *Mary Barnes* (1978); *Teendreams* (with Susan Todd, 1979) and *Entertaining Strangers* (1985), a community play first commissioned by Ann Jellicoe and the Colway Theatre Trust and adapted for performance at the National Theatre, London in 1987. He has written four plays for the Royal Shakespeare Company, for whom he acts as literary adviser: they are *Destiny* (1976); *The Jail Diary of Albie Sachs* (1978); *Nicholas Nickleby* (1980); and *Maydays* (1983). He received the John Whiting award for *Destiny,* the Society of West End Theatres best play award for *Nicholas Nickleby* (which also won him a Tony award in New York), and the Plays and Players best play award for *Maydays.* His television work includes adaptations of *Destiny, Jail Diary* and *Nicholas Nickleby,* and his first film, *Lady Jane,* was released in 1986.

Front cover: Photograph from first production by John Haynes
Back cover: David Edgar by Chris Davies

DAVID EDGAR

That Summer

A METHUEN PAPERBACK

A METHUEN MODERN PLAY

First Published in Great Britain as a paperback original in 1987
by Methuen London Ltd., 11 New Fetter Lane, London
EC4P 4EE and in the United States of America by Methuen
Inc., 29 West 35th Street, New York, NY 10001

Corrected reprint 1988

Set in IBM 10 point Journal by 𝔽 Tek Art Limited,
Croydon, Surrey
Printed by Richard Clay Ltd, Bungay, Suffolk

British Library Cataloguing in Publication Data

Edgar, David.
    That summer.
    I. Title
    822'.914   PR6055.D44

    ISBN 0-413-17450-6

To Stephen Oliver

That Summer was first performed at the Hampstead Theatre, London on 2 July 1987. The cast was as follows:

CRESSIDA, *early 30s, a chiropractor*	Jessica Turner
HOWARD, *early 40s, a university lecturer*	Oliver Cotton
DANIEL, *16, Howard's son by his first marriage*	Edward Rawle-Hicks
ALUN, *mid 30s, a miner*	Gareth Morris
MICHELE, *15, Alun's daughter*	Caroline Berry
FRANKIE, *15, Michele's friend*	Catherine Tregenna
TERRY, *mid-30s, a schoolteacher*	Mick Ford

Directed by Michael Attenborough
Designed by Sue Plummer
Lighting by Gerry Jenkinson

The play is set in a holiday house in North Wales, in August 1984.

The set consists of the living room of the house, and a terrace, connected (we imagine) by french windows. In the living room is a selection of fairly basic furniture, including easy chairs, a dining table and dining chairs.

There is a large vase on a side-dresser. On the terrace is a bench and table.

At the back of the living room are two doors: one leading to the hallway, the other to the kitchen and the other interior rooms of the house.

From the terrace, it is possible to walk down to the beach. We imagine an extension to the terrace on the same side.

Author's Note

The action of *That Summer* is set against the background of the 1984-5 miners' strike. The play is a work of fiction and its characters are invented. But it nonetheless owes much to many Rhondda miners and their families; in particular to Pat and John Bates and Tony and Maudie Gazzi; and most of all to their daughters Karen and Lisa.

David Edgar

ACT ONE

Scene One

On the terrace, the bench and table. Also, a canvas garden-chair, recliner, and a free-standing barbecue.
At first, CRESSIDA *is alone, with everything else in darkness. As she speaks, late afternoon sunlight lightens the terrace and the living-room.*
Indeed, the light is so bright that CRESSIDA, *who wears a somewhat tent-like Japanese kimono, looks over-dressed, an intruder from another time.*

CRESSIDA. In fact, it wasn't smaller. I mean, they say that when you go back to a childhood place, then everything looks smaller. But for me, this time, if anything, I saw the photograph enlarged.

DANIEL, CRESSIDA'*s sixteen-year-old step-son, throws back the hallway door, and strides in, with his suitcase and sports bag. He looks around.*

DANIEL. Oh, Jesus.

He drops his cases and walks back out.

CRESSIDA. I think, you see, it was a matter of perspective. Before, I'd never raised my eyes above the water line. Nothing mattered if it didn't wriggle and you couldn't catch it in a net.

CRESSIDA'*s husband* HOWARD *marches into the living room from the interior of the house. He carries a duplicated document — the owner's description of the house and its facilities. He looks round the living-room.*

HOWARD. I see.

He goes out.

CRESSIDA. Even the sun was by reflection. Just a shiny penny glinting in a rockpool.

HOWARD (*calling*). Cressida! I've found the master bedroom with twin beds and shower en-suite!

CRESSIDA. That's when there was a sun of course. Personally, I've never bought the sundrenched summers of our youth.

HOWARD. There's also what purports to be an annexe with bunk beds and put-u-up where we could put your little friends . . .

CRESSIDA. My memories are all of plastic wellingtons and pac-a-macs.

HOWARD. That's if Terry doesn't mind the 'vestibule'.

CRESSIDA. So this time, for the first time, I could look along the headland, to the village. Down the scrubby cliff-path, to the beach. And crumbs. The sky. The sea.

> CRESSIDA *drifts away as* HOWARD *and* DANIEL *re-enter, simultaneously, through their previous doors.* DANIEL *has two carrier-bags of food.*

HOWARD. Danny, you're up top. It claims to be an ample attic space, but I'm afraid it's more a sort of loft. Had we brought the cat, it would be hazardous to swing her.

DANIEL. Kitchen?

HOWARD (*points to the door to the interior*). Thataway.

> DANIEL *goes out towards the kitchen.* HOWARD *looks at the room.*

Well, by process of elimination, this must be the well-proportioned and attractive lounge with easy chairs, convertible settee and dining area.

> *He looks askance at the vase. He goes on the terrace. He looks at the document, and looks up.*

HOWARD. I would have thought 'verandah' should imply some class of canopy or awning. I'd call this 'terrace'. (*He glances at the document.*) If not 'patio'.

> HOWARD *goes back into the living room as* DANIEL *reappears.*

HOWARD. You found the kitchen?

DANIEL. Yes. The fridge is full.

HOWARD. Well, yes. It isn't very —

DANIEL. It is full of film.

HOWARD. And food.

DANIEL. And tennis balls.

HOWARD. Danny, you know, you may have seen, at Wimbledon, when they ask for new balls, and the ballboys go and take them from a kind of cabinet —

CRESSIDA enters from the hallway. She is dressed in a more summery fashion. She carries a case of wine.

DANIEL. It's Dan*iel.*

HOWARD. All right then, Dan*iel,* you may have seen at Wimbledon —

CRESSIDA. Where shall I put the wine?

HOWARD. Oh, in the kitchen. On the left.

CRESSIDA. Presumably there is a fridge.

HOWARD. Why don't you put it in the pantry for a moment?

CRESSIDA. Fine.

She's on her way.

DANIEL. Seeing as how the fridge is full of Howard's balls.

CRESSIDA. I'm sorry? What was that?

DANIEL. Because, you see, at *Wimbledon* —

CRESSIDA puts the wine down near the door.

CRESSIDA. Is full of *what*?

Slight pause.

HOWARD. All right. In the modest to minute refrigerator, there is a box of half a dozen tennis balls. And a small amount of photographic film. I would point out there is also a great deal of food. For instance, there are several plastic boxes stuffed with chops and ribs and other toothsome segments of dead animal, which have been gently marinading in a rich array of sauces, stocks and glazes all the way from Oxford, and which I intend to barbecue tonight.

CRESSIDA. Already marinading. That's my man.

HOWARD. In fact, I think I'll start the charcoal. In anticipation of the Minerettes' arrival.

He goes out on to the terrace, looking for a suitable spot.

DANIEL. The miner — who?

CRESSIDA. It's what your father calls our little guests. And it's what he mustn't call them when they're here.

HOWARD *has re-entered the room.*

HOWARD. Firelighters.

CRESSIDA *throws him a packet of firelighters.*

Ta.

HOWARD *goes out to continue his search. He finds a spot to the side of the house, which need not be visable, where he sets up and lights the barbecue.* CRESSIDA *has picked up the wine.*

CRESSIDA. Right then. The pantry.

DANIEL (*as a car door slams, off*). Cressida —

CRESSIDA. Oh, cripes. That can't be them.

She goes and looks through the hallway door. Then, to DANIEL:

Get Howard, will you, dear?

She looks round for somewhere to put the wine and puts it on the dining table. Then she hurries out into the hall. After a moment, DANIEL *goes on to the terrace and shouts:*

DANIEL. Hey, Howard! Dad!

HOWARD. Yes? What?

DANIEL. The Minerettes.

HOWARD. Yes, what about them?

DANIEL. They've apparently arrived.

HOWARD *quickly appears. He wears leather gauntlets. He goes into the house.*

HOWARD. They've what?

DANIEL (*following* HOWARD). And, pr'aps, now, someone will explain —

HOWARD (*a little impatient*). I'm sorry?

DANIEL. Why 'our little guests'.

Pause.

HOWARD. Well, 'apparently', they've found it difficult to place them.

DANIEL. Place them.

HOWARD. Yes. The boys will go alone, you see, but the girls insist they have a friend or confidante —

DANIEL. No, no. I *meant,* why have you asked two perfect strangers on your holiday at all?

HOWARD. Our holiday. You. Your father. And his wife.

As HOWARD *continues,* ALUN *enters. He carries two suitcases.*

Well, as it happens, it was her idea. Via her friend Terry. Who knows one of their fathers. Who's a miner.

DANIEL. Oh, of *course.*

HOWARD (*quite sharply*). And I don't know if they actually take the papers in this — seminary your mother's packed you off to, but since March there's been this coal strike —

ALUN. Well, so they say. But then again, you mustn't go believing everything they tell you in the papers.

CRESSIDA comes in with a radio-cassette player and another case.

HOWARD. Alun. This is Daniel, my son.

ALUN. Well, hello, Daniel. And you're Howard. Very pleased to meet you.

He puts out his hand to shake. HOWARD's *still got his gauntlet on.*

HOWARD. Barbecue. For which we hope you'll stay.

CRESSIDA. Indeed.

ALUN. Well, that's very kind of you, but I ought to get on really. I'm supposed to be in Preston by tonight. But the offer's most appreciated.

HOWARD. Drink, at least.

ALUN. A cup of tea'd go down marvellously well. Now, where's those girls?

HOWARD. Um, they can't have got —

CRESSIDA. Or even, there's some fizzy wine —

HOWARD. There is a rather classy Cava —

ALUN. Um, no. No, thanks. I think the bobbies got my registration, see, and at present they don't need much excuse.

HOWARD. Yes, of course. Now, Daniel, could you pop the kettle on?

CRESSIDA *picks up the case of wine and hands it to* DANIEL.

CRESSIDA. And put that in the pantry.

DANIEL *throws a look, but then he goes.* HOWARD *looks through the hallway door.*

I'm afraid that Terry's late. I don't know where —

ALUN. No matter.

HOWARD. Well, you say that, but he's got the salads.

CRESSIDA. So, shall we 'take tea on the terrace'?

ALUN. It would be a pleasure.

CRESSIDA *gestures to* ALUN, *who goes out on to the terrace. She's following, when she sees* HOWARD, *who has turned from the door and is slumped against the wall in a mock indication of total astonishment. During the following,* ALUN *looks out to sea, notices the smoke from the barbecue, and goes to look at it.*

CRESSIDA. Howard?

HOWARD. It's them.

CRESSIDA. Who's them?

HOWARD. The Minerettes. I mean, there's no dispute. They are precisely how I . . . There's a fair one, and a dark one, and they're wearing . . .

CRESSIDA. *Howard.*

A head pops round the door. It's MICHELE's.

MICHELE. Um — excuse me. Beg your pardon. But can we come in, please?

CRESSIDA. Oh, yes. Of course. Indeed.

MICHELE *turns to the other girl, not yet visible.*

MICHELE. See, I told you, it's okay.

MICHELE *and* FRANKIE *enter. They are both 15.*
MICHELE *wears a white T-shirt with the slogan* 'FRANKIE SAYS' *in big letters.* FRANKIE's *T-shirt says* 'RELAX'.

Um — I'm Michele. And this here's Frankie.

HOWARD. Goes to Hollywood.

MICHELE. No, really. That's her name.

CRESSIDA. And this is Howard.

MICHELE. And are you Cressida?

CRESSIDA. Well, Cressida. Or — Chris.

HOWARD. In fact.

CRESSIDA. And your father's on the terrace.

HOWARD. Or verandah.

DANIEL *comes in with the tea.*

CRESSIDA. And here's tea. Daniel: Michele and Frankie.

MICHELE. How d'you do?

She nudges FRANKIE.

FRANKIE. Hello.

Slight pause.

DANIEL. Hello.

DANIEL takes the tea out and puts it on the table on the terrace.

HOWARD. Right then.

HOWARD and CRESSIDA lead FRANKIE and MICHELE on to the terrace.

Everyone arrives as ALUN returns from the barbecue.

ALUN. Ah, there you are.

CRESSIDA. Please, do sit down.

MICHELE sits on the bench. FRANKIE was about to sit on one of the garden chairs, but notices this in the nick of time and sits by MICHELE. DANIEL sits on the recliner. HOWARD starts pouring the tea.

HOWARD. Does anybody not take sugar?

MICHELE. No. I mean — no sugar, thanks.

DANIEL. No milk or sugar.

HOWARD. Right.

Pause.

So — was your journey —

ALUN. Fine. Bit of a snarl-up, round Dolgellau.

HOWARD. Ah.

Pause.

CRESSIDA (*with a glance at the sky*). And is it, um — like this, down where you are?

ALUN. The weather? more or less.

Pause.

Now, Howard, is this right, I hear you're a historian?

HOWARD. Yes. Yes, I am.

ALUN. And are you, like . . . researching anything particular, at present?

HOWARD. Well, at this very moment, I'm, um, sort of moonlighting. I mean, I'm, by profession, I'm a don — a lecturer. But at this moment, as I say, I'm working for a television company. There's a series on the 30s, 'Red Decade', all that, and I'm helping with the episode about the British left and Spain. How people like John Strachey, Harold Laski, how they responded to the Civil War. George Orwell. People of that ilk.

ALUN. Well, you've picked the year for it.

HOWARD. Indeed. Though of course it won't go out in 1984. In fact, the notion is to coincide —

ALUN. Well, no, I meant the strike. Over a hundred South Wales miners fought in Spain, I'm proud to say.

HOWARD. Oh, yes, indeed. I'm sorry.

ALUN. No need to apologise.

HOWARD. A glorious chapter in your history.

ALUN. Well, if you like.

HOWARD. I mean, it must be — very close to you.

ALUN. Well, yes.

CRESSIDA. Were there any from your village?

Slight pause.

ALUN. Yes. I believe so. One or two.

Pause.

In fact, if I'm honest, what appeals to me, by way of history, goes much further back than that. In archaeology. The ruins of old cultures, crumbling into dust, then rediscovered after centuries. Like, the Book of Nahum. You know, Nineveh and Tyre.

CRESSIDA *smiles and shrugs.*

CRESSIDA. No chapel childhood, I'm afraid.

ALUN (*with a shrug*). No. School.

Pause.

HOWARD (*looks at his watch*). Now, look, I really ought to make a —

CRESSIDA. Come. We will watch Escoffier.

HOWARD. Momento.

HOWARD *goes out to the kitchen.*

ALUN. He's a dab hand at the cooking, is he, eh?

CRESSIDA. And needs to be. He made a foolish marriage. Wife can't boil an egg. Well, that's not absolutely true. The real disaster's scrambling. As he says, they tend to end up stood in peaks. Like the Grand Tetons.

ALUN. Sorry?

CRESSIDA. Mountains, in America.

HOWARD *has reappeared with a pile of plastic containers, plates, spatulas and other implements.*

HOWARD. Wyoming. (*To* DANIEL.) Bottom shelf is free.

DANIEL. *Thank* you.

HOWARD (*as he goes towards the barbecue*). You know, young Terence better not be too much longer.

CRESSIDA. Why?

HOWARD (*obvious*). He's bringing half the food.

CRESSIDA. Oh, yes.

HOWARD *goes out to the barbecue.*

You might say, just the weeniest bit obsessional. Like taking his own mayonnaise to restaurants. Banning Heinz tomato ketchup from the house.

CRESSIDA *gestures* ALUN *to go with her to the barbecue.* DANIEL *makes to go into the house.* CRESSIDA *gestures to him, indicating that he should stay and talk to the girls.* ALUN *and* CRESSIDA *go.* DANIEL *stands there. He drums the back of a chair with his fingers.*

DANIEL (*eventually*). Um — how was your journey?

MICHELE *and* FRANKIE *nod, smile and shrug.*

MICHELE. All right.

FRANKIE. Fine.

Pause.

DANIEL. You come from — South Wales as I gather. From the south.

MICHELE. Correct.

FRANKIE. You know — the valleys.

Pause.

DANIEL. Mm. The Rhondda.

His rounded, hard-d pronunciation pushes the girls over the edge. They crack up. DANIEL is furious.

Yes?

MICHELE. It's — Rhondda.

FRANKIE (*with an odd, offhand gesture*). Rhondda Valley.

DANIEL can take no more.

DANIEL. Right, then.

He strides out through the living room. FRANKIE and MICHELE look at each other, a shared moment. Then:

MICHELE. Hey, Frankie. D'you like, know where we are?

FRANKIE. I dunno. Gwynedd?

MICHELE. Oh.

Pause.

FRANKIE. Hey, Michele. You seen a telly?

MICHELE. No.

FRANKIE. Hey, s'pose they haven't got one? What the hell we going to do?

Pause.

MICHELE. I heard there's some got holidays in Georgia. You know, Russian Georgia.

MICHELE looks at FRANKIE. FRANKIE looks around.

FRANKIE. Some people, all the luck.

Enter CRESSIDA.

CRESSIDA. The latest news is dinner in ten minutes. If you want to wash or anything.

MICHELE *and* FRANKIE *nod and stand.*

MICHELE. Yes, please.

CRESSIDA (*looks round*). Um – Daniel!

DANIEL *comes into the living room from the kitchen.*

DANIEL. Yes?

CRESSIDA. I think the girls are in the 'annexe'.

DANIEL *goes to the interior door and opens it with a gesture.*

And their bags are there.

DANIEL *goes and picks up the bags.*

DANIEL. Pliz valk zis way, mamzelles.

FRANKIE *and* MICHELE *look at each other and follow* DANIEL *out.* ALUN *has re-entered with his tea. He nods back, in the direction of the barbecue.*

ALUN. Miraculous.

CRESSIDA. It keeps him off the streets.

She sits. ALUN *follows.*

So what's in Preston?

ALUN. There's a power station. Well, nearby, as I understand it. Place called Heysham.

CRESSIDA. Ah.

ALUN. Bringing the day closer when she's calling us 'the enemy within' by candlelight.

CRESSIDA. You think that's how it's going to end?

ALUN. It's going to end in victory.

CRESSIDA. No, I meant, *that way.* Industrially. By closing down the power stations. Stopping trains.

ALUN. Oh, there's no doubt about it, to my mind. It'll finish when the lights go out, like last time. That's my prediction.

CRESSIDA. Hence the trip to Heysham.

ALUN. Right.

CRESSIDA. Do you enjoy it? Picketing?

Pause.

ALUN. Well, it can be a bit boring. Or by contrast, p'raps a little over-hectic, on occasions. But by and large I'm having a great time.

CRESSIDA. The travel. And all that.

ALUN. Exactly. Bit of a – magical mystery tour, this strike, if you take my meaning. A temporary suspension of one's usual obligations.

CRESSIDA. Footloose and flying free.

ALUN. That's right.

ALUN's picked up a note in CRESSIDA's tone.

Now tell me. I'm not in the presence of a dreaded Oxford feminist, or am I?

Slight pause.

CRESSIDA. Sorry?

ALUN. You know, the dungarees and everybody's really lesbian brigade. Notorious throughout the length and breadth, they are.

CRESSIDA (*uncertain*). Um – may I ask, what makes you think –

ALUN. 'Footloose and Fancy Free.' You sounded as if you didn't quite approve.

CRESSIDA. Oh, no. That wasn't what I meant at all. (*Pause. Briskly.*) I mean, don't get me wrong. I mean, I kind of work and everything . . . But as far as being, dungarees . . . No, that stuff gets right up my nose. (*Slight pause.*) I mean, I collect food, for food parcels, outside supermarkets, and aside from the didactic dieticians, you know, tons of wholewheat pasta and no tins, apart from them, the ones who really irk

me are the women who give nothing that a man can use at
all. All baby food and tights and tampax. Which is of
course all very well and useful but — it seems to miss the
point. To me.

A head pops round the hall door. It belongs to TERRY. *He's
from Yorkshire. During the following he brings in his luggage
in two loads: the first is a suitcase and portable TV, the
second two large bowls with plates on top and a plastic
carrier-bag.*

ALUN. What do you do?

CRESSIDA. I'm sorry?

ALUN. When you kind of work.

CRESSIDA. Oh, I'm a sort of doctor.

ALUN. What sort?

CRESSIDA. Chiropractor.

ALUN. Pardon?

CRESSIDA. I do work on backs.

ALUN. What, like an osteopath?

CRESSIDA. Well, in that we manipulate. But osteopaths knock
you about more, and they tend to concentrate only on the bit
that's hurting, while we're more concerned with the whole
spine. Howard calls osteopathy chiropractic Marxist-Leninist.
The delusion that you can build socialism in one vertebra.

ALUN. Yes. I see. (*Slight pause.*) And is it Howard brought you
in to all of this?

CRESSIDA. What, to the strike? Oh, no. Well, not directly.

Slight pause.

No, in fact this time it's been more me.

TERRY. That's more you what?

CRESSIDA. Hey, Terry. Where d'you creep in from?

TERRY *comes on to the terrace with his carrier-bag.*

TERRY (*taking a bottle from his bag*). Beware of creeps bearing gifts.

CRESSIDA. Sambuca!

ALUN. Hello, Terry.

TERRY. Alun. I'm sorry I'm so late. The roadsigns are in Sanskrit.

HOWARD enters from the barbecue, carrying plates of cooked food, en route through the living room and out to the kitchen.

HOWARD. Well, he'd better have the salads. That's all *I* can say.

TERRY. Well, yes, in fact, and though I says it —

HOWARD. You got *five* from *now.*

He's gone.

TERRY. Well, hi there, Howard. (*To* CRESSIDA.) So. You two been forging links?

CRESSIDA. Alun's been telling me about the dreaded Oxford feminists.

TERRY. Ay, well. You've got to understand that Alun's what you might call a mite unreconstructed on the women question —

ALUN. Oh, come on now, Terry. I told you, all that fuss about the May Day rally? And we had to have equal speakers, male and female? And we must invite a gay and we've got to have a lesbian?

TERRY. See what I mean —

During the following HOWARD *enters the living room with plates and cutlery and starts laying the table.*

ALUN. One meeting, Cressida, I said the NCB was turning miners into what you might call industrial gypsies. And so half the fems jump up, saying, 'So, what's wrong with gypsies?' Apparently, I'm showing chauvinism to our gypsy brothers. Gypsy sisters. Well. Ridiculous, to my mind.

HOWARD *calls from the living room:*

HOWARD. Heartily agree.

ALUN. But you must have your supper.

CRESSIDA. No, really, we can have it any time . . .

A look from HOWARD, *who's passing back en route to the barbecue.*

ALUN. No, I should have been off already, anyway. I'll just go and tell the girls goodbye.

TERRY. Well, if you're sure . . .

CRESSIDA. I'll show you where they are.

She takes ALUN *through the living room and out.* TERRY'*s alone on the terrace. He goes and gets his casseroles, picks up a pair of wooden spoons from the table, and comes back out. He opens one of the casseroles — which contains potato salad — finds a screwtop jar in his carrier, opens it and dresses the salad with the contents, tossing with the wooden spoons.*

Enter DANIEL.

DANIEL. Terry.

TERRY. Danny.

DANIEL. Daniel. Did you bring the television?

TERRY. Yes.

DANIEL. Thank God for that. The Olympic track and field kicks off on Friday.

TERRY. Right.

HOWARD *crosses with another plate of barbecued food direct to the living-room table.*

HOWARD. Right then.

TERRY (*to* DANIEL). I think it's suppertime.

HOWARD. Just waiting for the salad monitor.

CRESSIDA *and* ALUN *come back into the living room.*

CRESSIDA. Well, they might have let you in.

ALUN. Oh, no. Can't interrupt the preparations.

CRESSIDA. What?

ALUN. Howard, you know, if you're studying the Spanish
    Civil War . . . You should ask Frankie how she got her name.
    If you get the chance.

HOWARD. Yes, sure. I will.

DANIEL and TERRY come into the living room.

ALUN. Well, then. Good luck with 'em. Don't take no nonsense,
    mind.

CRESSIDA. We won't.

TERRY. And give 'em hell at Heysham.

ALUN. Right.

HOWARD. Take care. It's good to meet you.

*DANIEL gives a little wave. ALUN goes to the hallway door.
He turns back.*

ALUN. Now, look. I know I don't have to tell you, but there's
    still lots of people talk as if this strike's about wages and
    conditions. Who don't understand that it's about survival.
    Not just for us, but for our kids. So they don't end up — well,
    you know. And to my mind, if we're going to stand a chance,
    we've got to show *we* can survive. So I hope it don't need
    saying. But, you know . . . How grateful we all are. (*Slight
    pause.*) 'Cos if not, she might as well just flood the valley,
    turn the bloody thing into a reservoir. In my opinion, anyway.

*Slight pause. He smiles, goes to TERRY and lightly punches
him on the shoulder. TERRY mirrors the gesture: clearly this
is a ritual.*

So. So long, our Terry. (*To the others.*)

All of you.

He goes.

CRESSIDA. She?

TERRY. Goes without saying.

CRESSIDA. Yuh.

Pause.

HOWARD. Right. Action. Daniel. There is souvlaki in the oven, dips and relishes are on a tray. Oh, and the wine.

CRESSIDA *is looking at the meat on the table.*

CRESSIDA. What's this?

DANIEL *goes out.* TERRY *collects his salads and brings them to the table.*

HOWARD. It's spareribs. What's it look like. Terry . . .

CRESSIDA. Howard . . .

TERRY (*putting his salads on the table*). Potato salad. Spinach.

CRESSIDA. . . . you are convinced . . .

HOWARD (*handing TERRY an empty serving plate*). Looks wonderful. There's chicken tikka on the barbecue.

CRESSIDA. . . . they'll actually *like* . . .

As TERRY *goes out,* DANIEL *comes in with the tray.*

DANIEL. Your meat. Your wine.

HOWARD. The girls.

DANIEL *turns round, hands the tray to* CRESSIDA *and goes back out.* HOWARD *puts the stuff from the tray on the table.*

CRESSIDA. . . . they'll actually eat this stuff?

Slight pause.

HOWARD. I'm sorry? What d'you mean?

CRESSIDA. You are convinced they'll eat the food.

HOWARD. Whyever not? (*Pause.*) Why, what do you think they'd like?

CRESSIDA. Well, burgers, I'd imagine. Hot dogs. Things like that.

HOWARD. This establishment does not serve things like that.

Enter TERRY *with chicken tikka, still on skewers, on the plate.*

CRESSIDA. Would you say that about culture? Would you say they can't have Coronation Street, they must have Turandot?

TERRY (*putting down the plate, to* HOWARD). Your move.

HOWARD. Coronation Street is part of a genuine popular narrative tradition.

CRESSIDA. Well, Crossroads.

HOWARD. Arguably just the same.

CRESSIDA. The Price is Right.

HOWARD. They will have pork ribs in Hoisin sauce and like it. (DANIEL *comes in during*:) Look, just because their fathers are on strike, you treat them as if they're refugees. They are perfectly normal, no doubt actually fairly average, contemporary teenage girls —

DANIEL. Ahem.

He gestures theatrically to the door, through which come FRANKIE *and* MICHELE. *They have dressed up for dinner, and look quite extraordinary. In particular,* MICHELE's *hair is in spikes, and* FRANKIE's *a frightening new shade. They stand there.*

CRESSIDA. Well . . . Hi there. Supper. Hope you like barbecue.

The girls sit at the table, noting the television.

Now, this is Terry. Have you met?

They nod.

TERRY. We've briefly met.

CRESSIDA. And would you . . . like some wine?

They nod. Everyone else sits. Wine is poured.

And . . . chicken tikka?

They look bemused at the skewers.

HOWARD. It is mildly curried.

They shake their heads.

TERRY. Spareribs? You eat them with your fingers.

FRANKIE *and* MICHELE *look at each other and shake their heads. The souvlaki has been de-threaded.*

CRESSIDA. Um — grilled lamb?

MICHELE *takes a very small piece of lamb.* FRANKIE *does the same.*

Potato salad? Spinach?

They take small portions and hand the casseroles on. As the conversation continues, everyone else helps themselves, pulling pieces of chicken off the skewers, and munching the ribs in their fingers. Part of the problem for MICHELE *and* FRANKIE *has been not knowing how much to take, so as the others serve themselves with ample portions they glance at each other.*

CRESSIDA. It was nice to meet your dad, Michele. After all we've heard from Terry.

HOWARD. I was very glad to hear that he's refused to be transfixed by the loopier outreaches of Oxonian feminism.

CRESSIDA. What reaches, Howard?

HOWARD. Well, while he was talking, I was thinking about your buddy Hobbes.

CRESSIDA. She's not my buddy and her name isn't Hobbes.

HOWARD. I imagine Terry knows the type. Permanently furious at what she assumes you're going to say next.

TERRY. Why do you call her Hobbes?

CRESSIDA. You only don't like her 'cos she's so overt.

HOWARD. The latest outrage was a friend of mine, whose marriage broke up, and whose ex was charmed into the Hobbesian embrace — I don't think literally — but who accused my mate, when he wanted access to their child, of — wait for it — 'biologism'. (*Pause.*) She affects poverty. She ought to be in solitary. And she is indisputably nasty, brutish and short.

Pause.

TERRY. So what you up to, Danny?

DANIEL *about to correct him.*

Daniel.

DANIEL. Nothing much.

HOWARD. We're at present into bodies beautiful.

TERRY. Oh, whose?

HOWARD. Our own.

CRESSIDA. He's training.

TERRY. Right.

HOWARD. A project which appears to justify the daily calorific intake of a smallish Indian village for a year.

CRESSIDA (*to* MICHELE *and* FRANKIE). And presumably you two have just done CSEs?

MICHELE. O level.

CRESSIDA. Right. And how d'you think you've done?

MICHELE. Dunno. Okay.

CRESSIDA. And — what are your favourite subjects?

Pause.

MICHELE. Well, as it happens, I like history best.

CRESSIDA. Well, there's a hap—

MICHELE. But Frankie, she likes English Lit. Now don't you, Frankie?

Pause.

FRANKIE (*very quietly*). Yes. I do.

Pause.

HOWARD. So what . . . What books, particularly?

MICHELE *gesturing and encouraging* FRANKIE *through the sentence.*

FRANKIE. Well. I did like 'Romeo and Juliet'. And 'David Copperfield'. And the selected poems of John Keats.

Pause.

HOWARD (*to* FRANKIE). And after your results, what then?

Pause.

FRANKIE. Well, we'll be back at home.

HOWARD. No, I meant, you know, what does the future hold?

FRANKIE *looks round in panic.*

FRANKIE. Uh, I —

MICHELE (*suddenly*). Now, *my* ambition lies in archaeology.

Slight pause.

HOWARD. I'm sorry?

MICHELE. I have always been, like, fascinated by the history of ancient times.

CRESSIDA. What, like your dad?

MICHELE. Correct.

HOWARD. Well you've come to the right place. We'll hotfoot it to a castle or a monastery first thing.

MICHELE. I would like that very much.

TERRY. So what's it really like?

MICHELE. Beg pardon?

TERRY. What's it really like for you? I mean, it must be pretty tough. (*Pause.*) With no new clothes. No records. Treats. It must be hard.

MICHELE (*aggressively*). Well, we're not starving, anyway. (*Pause.*) I mean, those things, they're not important. So, we had to send the video back, but the house is still kept nice and tidy. It's not like we're in, you know, real poverty.

TERRY. What do you mean by that?

MICHELE. I mean, it's not like no one taking proper care of things. It's not like scrawling on the walls and business in the lifts and water coming through the roof and everybody lying round on pot and heroin. I mean, we've not descended to that level. We're not tramps or thieves. We've kept our pride.

Pause. FRANKIE kicks out her feet. She wears pink trainers which, now we notice them, look a bit odd with the rest of her outfit.

FRANKIE. Well, here they are.

TERRY. What's that?

FRANKIE. Me mam bought me new trainers for the holiday. Last new things till we won. (*Pause.*) Look silly with this, really.

Pause.

CRESSIDA. Look. Do have some more. (*Pause.*) We don't want anyone to think we're starving you . . .

TERRY *helps himself to a large helping of potato salad and then hands it to* MICHELE *and* FRANKIE.

TERRY. Go on.

FRANKIE *helps herself.* MICHELE *helps herself.* TERRY *helps himself to spareribs and passes them. Again, they help themselves to large helpings. Following* TERRY, *they pick the ribs up with their fingers and eat.*

Blackout.

Scene Two

The following week. Morning. In the living room, the television is set up on a small table, the radio-cassette is on the floor, surrounded by cassettes and presently playing the morning news in Welsh. We hear words like 'Sheffield', 'Arthur Scargill', 'N.U.M.', 'Los Angeles' and 'Daley Thompson'. On the table is the first 'load' of breakfast crockery and cutlery. CRESSIDA *enters from the interior side, in her dressing gown. She looks a little furtive. She goes to the big vase, feels in it, and takes out a small transparent plastic cube with some mechanism inside. She's about to go back out when she hears voices. She quickly goes out on to the terrace and hurries round the side of the house.* HOWARD *and* DANIEL *enter from the kitchen with cereals, fruit juice and coffee.*

HOWARD *wears tennis whites and* DANIEL *wears running gear. He has a walkman — the phones are presently round his neck. As they argue,* HOWARD *switches off the radio, pours cereal and*

coffee, and takes them through on to the terrace, followed by
DANIEL, *who contents himself with orange juice.*

DANIEL. I mean, Duran fucking Duran.

HOWARD. I'm sorry?

DANIEL. What?

HOWARD. The reference escapes me. Duran who?

DANIEL. They purport to be a pop group.

HOWARD. There's a group called Duran fuck—

DANIEL (*imitating the girls*). And 'I got the latest Wham
    cassette, d'you wanna hear it, Daniel' and 'Oh no I can't go
    swimming with my skin, it blisters something dreadful' and
    'Ooh Terry, you'll have to help me round the battlements,
    I got this terrible vertigo' and that's not to mention all those
    hours in the bathroom and the constant getting ready and
    'Ooh don't you like Duran Duran, Daniel, I think they're
    really great —'

HOWARD. You're only peeved about the castle because Michele
    knew King John preceded all the Edwards.

DANIEL. That's just not fair. What I found peeving was —

HOWARD. In fact, she appeared to have remarkable command of
    the epoch as a whole.

DANIEL. If you want to know, I'm peeved because I don't know
    why they're here. And I don't know why *I'm* here. At all.

Enter CRESSIDA, *with all the insouciance of someone whose
last entrance was successfully undiscovered. She wears a
colourful, vertically striped T-shirt, long French-type shorts
and tennis shoes.*

HOWARD. You're here because your mother's in New York.

DANIEL. Not for two weeks.

HOWARD. And because she thinks the three of *us* should get a
    little closer.

DANIEL. Ha!

Pause.

CRESSIDA. Frankie's agreed to doubles. Could you wake them, please?

After a slight pause, DANIEL *turns to* HOWARD.

DANIEL. Howard, what does your dear wife think she's wearing?

CRESSIDA. Um —

DANIEL. I'll go wake Frankie.

He goes into the living room. He's on his way to the interior door, when he sees the cassette player and cassettes. During the following, he inserts two or three cassettes into his walkman, so he can test what they are without being overheard. The first he rejects. The second he looks at quizzically, and pockets. The third he smiles at, takes out of the walkman, puts in the cassette player. He picks up the player and goes out. This process can take up to TERRY's *entrance.*

HOWARD. One sees his point.

CRESSIDA. I'm dressed for tennis.

HOWARD. No, you're not. You may be dressed in what you plan to wear to play the game, but dressed for it you're unequivocally not.

CRESSIDA. Howard, it is a recrea—

HOWARD. Rather like those students I remember who thought that wearing dirty jeans and odd socks proved their proletarian credentials, whereas, in fact, the real working class —

CRESSIDA. Howard. Don't take him out on me.

Enter TERRY *from the beach. He's been swimming, and wears a beachrobe. He breathes.*

HOWARD. Good morning, Terry.

TERRY. Morning. You know, all in all, gravity's a mixed blessing. Is that breakfast?

He goes into the living room and gets breakfast. HOWARD *follows.*

HOWARD. Terry, the court is booked at ten.

TERRY. Ah, yes. Now, Howard, I'm not sure —

HOWARD. Terry, it's taken a week of patient negotiation —

TERRY (*pouring coffee*). Sure, I know, it's just I think I may have pulled —

Suddenly, very loud music, DANIEL *shouting, and even the odd shriek from* FRANKIE *and* MICHELE. CRESSIDA *comes into the room.*

DANIEL (*off*). Wake up! Wake up! Show a leg there! Eight bells called! Bring out yer dead! Awake!

TERRY. What the hell —

CRESSIDA. It's Daniel. I asked him to —

DANIEL enters with the cassette player still blaring. He switches it off.

DANIEL. Girls woken. I'm off running. Tra.

He puts down the cassette player, puts on his earphones, and goes out to the hall.

CRESSIDA. What's wrong with him?

HOWARD goes out to the terrace with CRESSIDA, *followed by* TERRY.

HOWARD. His mother's just back from Manhattan. He's in Gwynedd. What d'you think?

TERRY. What's with the Dani*el*?

HOWARD. He was born in 1968.

That's not a total answer.

Danny Cohn Bendit. Paris. May events.

That's still not an explanation.

I think, you could say, he's engaging in a heartfelt but inchoate act of protest —

TERRY. Right.

HOWARD. He should be glad we didn't call him Stokeley or Fidel.

CRESSIDA. Or Peace or Love or Freedom.

TERRY. And do we yet know why Frankie's Frankie?

CRESSIDA. No. I tried to ask. But she doesn't seem to want to say.

Slight pause.

TERRY (*mock conspiratorial*). I'll get her on her own.

MICHELE *and* FRANKIE *enter.* FRANKIE *wears a skirt and sports shirt, but not matching.*

MICHELE. Good morning, all.

CRESSIDA. Hi, girls. Do you want some breakfast?

MICHELE. Not for me.

FRANKIE *goes and gets cereal.* MICHELE *puts on her dark glasses as she comes out on to the terrace.*

TERRY. But . . . But . . . You're *beautiful* –

MICHELE. Oh, Terry!

CRESSIDA (*looking at the weather*). Well, can this last, I ask myself.

TERRY. No problem. Weatherwise, we have it absolutely sorted.

HOWARD. How?

TERRY. The slightest puff of cloud appears, we sacrifice Michele.

MICHELE. Oh, you . . .

FRANKIE *appears with her cereal.*

FRANKIE. Oh, I didn't know we'd got to dress up like.

Slight pause.

CRESSIDA. Whereas of course the *real* working class –

HOWARD. It's all right, Frankie. You look absolutely fine. Particularly beside Cressida, who has misread the invitation yet again and come as a deckchair.

TERRY. Or a stick of rock.

HOWARD. Not from this angle.

CRESSIDA. Actually, I think I might, on this one, take a rain check.

HOWARD. Some day that phrase will be explained to me.

CRESSIDA. I mean, if Terry's pulled his — well, I hardly like to ask —

TERRY (*to* MICHELE). My lips are sealed.

CRESSIDA. Then why don't you play singles?

Pause.

HOWARD. Yes, why not. I'll get my racket.

He goes into the living room, followed by CRESSIDA *and* FRANKIE.

CRESSIDA. Frankie can use mine. It's got a thinner grip than Daniel's.

HOWARD *goes to the kitchen, returning with tennis balls and his racket, as* CRESSIDA *gives* FRANKIE *her racket and* MICHELE *and* TERRY *converse.*

TERRY. Are you going to go?

MICHELE. Oh, sure.

TERRY. You needn't.

MICHELE. Oh, I couldn't let her go *alone.*

FRANKIE (*calls*). You ready then, Michele?

MICHELE (*to* TERRY). 'My lips are sealed.'

TERRY. No one need ever know.

MICHELE. Oh, *you*!

MICHELE *goes into the living room with* HOWARD *and* FRANKIE. *The three go, as*:

HOWARD. Now, in fact, you'll notice that my forehand's rather weak, which is because I pulled a shoulder while of all things mounting tiles . . .

As soon as they're gone, CRESSIDA *hurries quickly out to the kitchen.* TERRY *notices. He stands, looking into the living room.*

TERRY. Cressida? Chris?

CRESSIDA *appears again. She is affecting unconcern.*

CRESSIDA. Well. Peace.

TERRY. Mm.

CRESSIDA *joins* TERRY *on the terrace. She sits on the recliner, lies back in the sun.*

CRESSIDA. So how's your — strain?

TERRY. Well, it could do with some attention.

CRESSIDA. Oh? Like what?

TERRY. Gi'us a massage then, chuck.

CRESSIDA (*shocked*). No.

TERRY. What's this? Professional reticence?

CRESSIDA. Terry. I am a chiropractor. Not a Swedish —

TERRY. Oh, come come. The magic fingers.

Pause.

CRESSIDA. Very well. Lie down and think of Islington.

TERRY *takes off his beachrobe and lies on it on the table.* CRESSIDA *gets up and goes and massages his back.*

TERRY. So how's it going?

CRESSIDA. Oh, fine, I think, don't you? Daniel is being pretty bolshie, but I think . . . he would be anyway. And the gels are starting to come out at last.

TERRY. You mean, socially? Or is Frankie finding hidden urges —

CRESSIDA. I can't understand why on earth they find you funny. All your jokes are way beneath their level.

TERRY. It may be that the alternatives are Howard's.

CRESSIDA. Howard is very droll. It's just his taste in humour has to be acquired.

TERRY. If not contracted. No, I meant — how is your strain?

Pause.

CRESSIDA. I see no reason to revise my answer. Fine.

TERRY. The academic life? The constant sherry?

CRESSIDA. Well, just listen to the darling dodo. Lapsang Souchong. Perrier.

TERRY. And living in North Oxford?

CRESSIDA. Smashing.

TERRY. You're serious?

CRESSIDA. Crumbs, yes. Over half the population suffers from some form of chronic inflammation of the lumbar spine — they claim it's poring over their word processors but I blame all that bicycling. My acupuncturist and I met on our basic Alexander course, we read the Tarot on our nights off, and I'm blissfully content.

TERRY. And do you see — the former Mrs —

CRESSIDA. Gillian? Not often. Met her, obviously. She's big in TV movies. Package, deal and megabuck.

TERRY. So did she get Howard this — this telly thing?

CRESSIDA. No, not directly. Look, who's doing this? The masseur asks the questions. Not the massagee.

TERRY. Well, just the one.

CRESSIDA. I need only give name, rank and number.

TERRY. Why did you run off to the kitchen when they'd gone?

Pause.

CRESSIDA. Just now?

TERRY. Uh-huh.

CRESSIDA. My test is in the pantry.

TERRY. Eh? What test?

CRESSIDA. For what. For pregnancy.

Pause.

TERRY. Congratulations?

CRESSIDA *shakes her head.*

TERRY. Why, wouldn't Howard —

CRESSIDA. No, not wouldn't. Couldn't.

TERRY. Pardon?

CRESSIDA. On account of his vasectomy.

Pause.

TERRY. Um . . . Do you know . . . ?

CRESSIDA. Oh, just about. I mean, I've narrowed it down to half a dozen.

TERRY. Sorry.

CRESSIDA. Awful irony. It was the strike. A talent contest. At some social. Quite excruciating. And eventually, escaped. In the most delightful company. (*Pause.*) He's a sort of Trot at Cowley. Lovely fella. Lovely time.

TERRY. It's over?

CRESSIDA. It has — run it's natural course. Or at least, I thought it had. (*She realises she's stopped her massage.*) I'm sorry. Where was I?

TERRY sits up.

TERRY. So what's the news?

CRESSIDA. Dunno. You've got to leave it for an hour, undisturbed, for the hormone or whatever to react. I did one Tuesday, actually, but it seemed to have got jolted when we put the cereals away.

TERRY looks bemused.

You see, the only place that I could think to put it was the pantry shelf.

TERRY. The pantry —

CRESSIDA. Cool and dry. But naturally, concealed. Behind the fettucini.

TERRY. Cressida.

CRESSIDA. Yes, Terence?

TERRY. Had . . . Had Howard had, was Howard, when you married him . . . ?

CRESSIDA. Oh, yes. (*Pause.*) You see, I didn't . . . don't want babies. And they refuse to do the operation if you haven't had one. Absolutely. No exception. So Howard was the perfect choice. In every way.

TERRY. You mean, you chose to abrogate your right to choose.

Pause.

CRESSIDA. Yes. I suppose so. Yes. In fact. As I watch the thundering stampede of what-me-nevers rushing to get their ankles through the stirrups, before they hit the danger zone, you know, thirty-eight or nine . . . Yes, I wanted a locked door behind me. No internal catch. An − an irrevocable decision.

Pause.

TERRY. And now?

CRESSIDA. Oh, absolutely. On that question, there is none.

TERRY. And on the other one?

She smiles, squeezes his shoulder, stands, moves away. TERRY *sits up. She looks back.*

CRESSIDA. Look. (*Slight pause.*) It is important, Terry, that you understand about my husband. When we met. For he was wonderful. I mean, I really hadn't done a thing − I'd been on half a dozen marches, I suppose, done some street theatre . . . But he'd done it all. Knew everything. And could do, anything. So clever, so experienced, committed, *clear* . . .

TERRY. So what went wrong?

Pause.

CRESSIDA. Dunno. (*Pause.*) I *do* know. That since − this little thing about which we will drop no hint however slight of any kind to anyone, that since that, I've been flying free. In a way I haven't been for years. And it is − magical.

Pause.

TERRY. Well. We'll keep 'em crossed then, eh?

DANIEL *runs round the side of the house, on to the terrace. He comes to a halt, bends over and breathes heavily.*

Hi there, Daniel.

DANIEL. Well — at least I beat them up the road.

CRESSIDA. Beat who?

DANIEL. Howard. The Minerettes.

CRESSIDA. Already?

DANIEL. Right. I'm going to have my shower.

He goes into the living room. Seeing the cassette player, he remembers something. He checks his pocket, finds he still has the cassette he took earlier, picks up the recorder and takes it through the interior door.

TERRY. In fact, though, if you think about it, there's something pretty bizarre about calling your child Cressida.

CRESSIDA. It was a pun. Ironically enough. I was the result of what was incorrectly thought a false alarm.

TERRY. 'As false as Cressida'.

CRESSIDA. You got it.

TERRY. No wonder you're at home.

CRESSIDA (*looks at her watch*). Ah. Which reminds me —

She's going through into the living room as HOWARD, FRANKIE and MICHELE come in from the outside.

So. How went the day?

She looks to HOWARD, who gestures to FRANKIE. FRANKIE waves her arms, a little gauchely.

FRANKIE. I won, I won.

HOWARD. She's very good.

FRANKIE. Oh, it was luck, mind. Howard's shoulder. Stuff like that.

HOWARD. That's true. But I'm certain, if you took some lessons, got your backhand sorted out, you could be really . . .

He realises FRANKIE'*s face has fallen.*

FRANKIE. Lessons. Well.

HOWARD. I mean, to firm up your technique, I didn't mean —

FRANKIE. Thanks for the game.

She goes off into the interior of the house.

HOWARD (*to* MICHELE). What's wrong?

TERRY. I think, it may be, that they can't afford —

MICHELE (*improvising*). I think, you know, you sounded like her mother. I think that's what upset her. Think you sound like her.

HOWARD. 'What you need is some nice chicken soup'.

MICHELE. Beg your pardon?

HOWARD. It's a joke. This guy says to his shrink — psychiatrist — doctor, 'I seem to think that everyone's my mother.' Shrink replies: 'Don't worry. What you need is some nice chicken soup.'

MICHELE'*s face is frozen into an expression of pleasurable anticipation.* CRESSIDA *looks to* TERRY, *who moves in.*

TERRY. Or even — there's the guy who's spent his whole life searching for the meaning of the universe . . .

CRESSIDA *isn't sure this is a good idea.*

CRESSIDA. Ah. Now, perhaps —

But MICHELE *has transferred her attention — and expression — to* TERRY.

TERRY. . . . and his search takes him all over, and eventually he hears that there is but one person in the world who knows the total meaning of the universe, this guru on this mountain in Tibet.

TERRY *pauses, impressively.* CRESSIDA, *prompting, to hurry it along.*

CRESSIDA. And so, sells up his business, mortgages his house . . .

TERRY. . . . that's right, he sacrifices everything, and sets off to seek this mountain . . .

CRESSIDA. . . . finds it, climbs it . . .

TERRY. . . . thank you, yes, and at the top there is this little
wizened man, and he, the guy, says, 'Oh great guru, I'm
reliably informed you know the meaning of the universe, the
answer to all questions,' and the old guy says, 'That's right, I
do, the answer to the question of the meaning of the universe
is simple. It is "chicken soup".'

Pause. MICHELE *doesn't move a muscle.*

And the guy says, 'You old bastard. I have spent my whole life
searching for the secret of the universe, I've sold up everything
I own, I've trekked across the world, I've climbed this fucking
mountain, and you have the nerve, the immortal gall, rind and
temerity to tell me that the answer's *chicken soup*?'

MICHELE *has stopped breathing.*

And the guru says, 'You mean it isn't chicken soup?' (*With a
little music-hall gesture:*)

Bu-boom.

Everybody laughs.

HOWARD. Well, it's good to greet old friends.

Holding up his box of tennis balls.

Now, yielding to not inconsiderable pressure, I shall put these
in the pantry.

HOWARD *goes out to the kitchen.* CRESSIDA *has got the
giggles, which* MICHELE *is finding mildly infectious.*

TERRY (*to* MICHELE). It's the way I tell 'em.

CRESSIDA'*s laughter propels her on to an easy chair.*

Well, it wasn't — quite, that . . .

CRESSIDA. No, it's not your stupid joke . . . It's just that
Howard's going to put his balls . . . in a cool . . . dry . . .

Suddenly she realises where HOWARD'*s going to put his balls.*

Crikey.

She's on her feet when MICHELE *starts her contribution.*
CRESSIDA *is captured in the glare.*

MICHELE. There's this poof, see, who comes back from the
office, right, and there's his friend, you know, sitting with his
bottom in the fridge. And the first poof says, 'Hey, what you
doing with your bottom in the fridge? And the second poof
says 'Well I thought, that after a hard day' . . .

TERRY. . . . 'you'd want something cool to slip into.'

MICHELE (*with* TERRY's *gesture*). Bu-boom. (*To* CRESSIDA.)
He knew it.

CRESSIDA. Sorry.

She runs to the door, just as HOWARD *comes through it. He
is very exercised.*

HOWARD. Cressida —

He sees MICHELE.

MICHELE. Well, I'd better — go and see to . . .

She hurries out.

HOWARD. Cressida. I have to talk to you.

CRESSIDA. Oh — yes?

TERRY. Um, should I — ?

CRESSIDA. Don't you dare.

HOWARD. It's a — what one might call the ultimate, loco-parental
nightmare.

CRESSIDA. What? Parental?

HOWARD. Look, the fact is, one of them appears to be —

FRANKIE *and particularly* MICHELE *start screaming off.*

What's that?

The door bursts open and DANIEL *enters followed by*
MICHELE *and* FRANKIE. DANIEL *has the cassette player,
on which is playing the cassette he listened to and pocketed
earlier, which is — as we will discover later — a tape made by*
MICHELE. MICHELE *is desperate to get the machine, and*

FRANKIE *is eager to help. The chase goes round the room, over the furniture, and culminates on the terrace.*

MICHELE. You give that back. Just give that back, Daniel —

CRESSIDA. Now, what's going on?

FRANKIE. Come on now, Daniel, give it to Michele.

HOWARD. For heaven's sake —

MICHELE. You bastard. Give that back. It's private.

TERRY. Frankie, what is —

DANIEL. No!

MICHELE. You fucking *bastard.*

FRANKIE (*explanatory*). Her cassette, you see . . .

The chase has reached the terrace. HOWARD *realises the phone has been ringing.*

HOWARD. What's that?

CRESSIDA. The phone. Remember — telephones?

HOWARD. Where is it?

TERRY. Kitchen.

HOWARD *runs out to the kitchen, as* MICHELE *corners* DANIEL *and starts hitting his chest, as* DANIEL *holds the recorder over his head.*

MICHELE. Bastard. Shit. Give it here. Give — it — to — me —

TERRY. Stop that, Michele.

Somewhat surprisingly, MICHELE *stops hitting* DANIEL.

Now, everyone, calm down. Michele, leave Daniel. Daniel, give me the machine.

MICHELE *leaves* DANIEL. DANIEL *hands the machine to* TERRY, *who switches it off.*

Now. What is this?

FRANKIE. It's a cassette. It's something Michele wrote. About the castle. It's a poem.

TERRY. Right. So it's Michele's.

He hands it to MICHELE.

CRESSIDA. I'd like to hear it.

MICHELE *looks alarmed.* TERRY *shakes his head.*

I'd like to hear it, please.

Pause. FRANKIE *takes the recorder from* MICHELE, *rewinds and plays*:

MICHELE'S VOICE (*on tape*).
The castle stands upon the hill,
In ruins now, all stark and still.
But as we mount its towers high,
We can imagine days gone by,
And how it must have been to climb
These high steep steps in Arthur's time,
And on the battlements catch sight
Of the shadow of a noble knight,
Or on a turret faintly hear
The voice of Launcelot or Guinevere.

MICHELE *gestures to* FRANKIE *to switch the tape off. But* FRANKIE *doesn't get to the button in time to miss*:

MICHELE'S VOICE. This poem's for Terry.

FRANKIE *switches the tape off.*

CRESSIDA. Thank you. That was very nice.

MICHELE. The last line doesn't match.

CRESSIDA. It doesn't scan. It doesn't matter.

She hands the machine to MICHELE.

There.

MICHELE *takes the machine. She and* FRANKIE *go out through the living room.* CRESSIDA *turns to look at* DANIEL. DANIEL *is about to say something, but changes his mind, and goes out as* HOWARD *re-enters the living room, carrying a paper bag.* TERRY *and* CRESSIDA *go into the living room.*

HOWARD. So what was all that?

CRESSIDA. Tell you later.

HOWARD (*taking the plastic cube — a pregnancy testing kit — from the bag and handing it to* CRESSIDA). Now look, Cressida, correct me if I'm wrong, but isn't this —

CRESSIDA. A pregnancy predictor.

HOWARD. Yes. (*Pause.*) So one of them is pregnant. Here.

TERRY. Well, they won't have actually *got* pregnant —

During this, CRESSIDA *takes the kit from* HOWARD *and looks at it. In fact, of course, it's been so jogged about that it's useless, but she makes great play of looking in the little mirrored surface at the bottom for the telltale ring.*

HOWARD. Yes, you see, it's wonderfully romantic, take a pair of utter strangers with us on holiday, being daughters of the revolutionary masses, as it were, but in the real world they are actually female adolescents at a particularly tricky age —

CRESSIDA. They are not pregnant.

HOWARD. What?

CRESSIDA. I've had these things before. Neither Michele nor Frankie has one in the oven.

HOWARD. Are you sure?

As HOWARD *looks impotently at the kit,* CRESSIDA *is able to shrug at* TERRY, *to indicate she can't tell the result.*

CRESSIDA. Well no doubt, in a day or two, there will be a confirmation.

HOWARD. Good. Well, I'm sure they'll be relieved.

CRESSIDA. I'll bet.

TERRY. It might be better if they didn't know we know.

HOWARD. Indeed.

He puts the test back in the bag, and makes to go.

CRESSIDA. What was the call?

HOWARD. The programme.

CRESSIDA. Good news?

HOWARD. Don't know. They want me to go back.

CRESSIDA. What for?

HOWARD. A meeting. Day after tomorrow.

CRESSIDA. That's Saturday.

HOWARD. Apparently these people work on Saturdays.

CRESSIDA. Didn't you explain you were on holiday?

HOWARD. Of course. But this is a very long, expensive series, and they will pay me to come back, and this is how these things occur.

CRESSIDA. You mean, in the zippy, zappy world of package, deal and megabuck.

HOWARD. Apparently.

He makes to go.

CRESSIDA. A world I worry you could learn to love.

Pause. TERRY delicately removes himself to the terrace, where he sits.

Oh, not the tinsel and jargon and the hype. But perhaps the zip and crackle. Getting on with it. Not loafing round the place complaining about everything. Operating in the real world.

Pause.

HOWARD. It is — it is very refreshing, sometimes, to be with people whose reaction to an ill-run whelkstall is to try and run it better. Who when they see a brewery, say, 'They're on me.' Who if they found themselves inside a paper bag, would seek not for excuses but the exit. (*Slight pause.*) Or if they came across an egg, think, hey, wow, I wonder how you cook this thing.

CRESSIDA. As opposed to oddballs taking strangers' kids on holiday. As opposed to trying to save an industry that in the real world —

HOWARD. I didn't say that.

CRESSIDA. Didn't even think it, shouldn't wonder. But it might be — what you feel. (*Long pause.*) Well, if you're off, tomorrow? . . . (HOWARD *nods.*) . . . let's have something nice tonight. I'm sure you boys can fix up something really scrumptious.

She goes off towards her room. HOWARD *comes out on to the terrace.* TERRY *looks up, not sure what* HOWARD's *going to do or say.*

HOWARD. Lobster. Lobster Thermidor.

Blackout.

Scene Three

Evening. CRESSIDA, HOWARD, TERRY, MICHELE *and* FRANKIE *sit round the dining table, which has been cleared after dinner. The girls are dressed up, the adults have changed — but are dressed informally. Everyone has wine.* TERRY *stands.*

TERRY. Comrades, I give you the complete and total victory of the National Union of Mineworkers, their struggle for their pits and their communities . . .

CRESSIDA. Hear hear.

MICHELE. Hear hear.

TERRY. And the utter rout of the armed might of the ruling class and its lackeys in the National Coal Board . . .

CRESSIDA. Boo! Boo!

FRANKIE. Boo.

HOWARD. That's not to mention all reactionaries, who as we know are paper tigers.

TERRY. I am content to toss in all reactionaries.

CRESSIDA. Running dogs.

TERRY. Them too. So, victory to the miners, utter rout of the forces of reaction —

HOWARD. The eternal friendship of our two great peoples —

TERRY. Natch —

DANIEL *comes in with a tray of coffee.*

CRESSIDA. And of course the chefs, for all the toothsome fare —

TERRY. So I should think —

FRANKIE. And Daniel, for making coffee —

TERRY. Daniel, especially, for coffee *and the rest* . . . But most of all — to us.

ALL. To us.

Everybody drinks. TERRY *and* DANIEL *sit. Coffee is distributed.*

CRESSIDA. Oooh, but he makes a pretty toast.

TERRY. Well, it's all those weddings.

HOWARD. Weddings?

TERRY. Oh, ay. You demonstrate an aptitude, you end up losing rings for half the village. I have read more telegrams in function room up at t'welfare —

FRANKIE. Welfare?

TERRY. Mm.

FRANKIE. You mean, like, miners' welfare?

TERRY. Yuh.

MICHELE. Well, fancy that.

TERRY. Yuh, my father was a deputy. South Yorks. Though, as it happens, I was born in Durham, and he'd been born in Lothian. Gypsies, tramps . . .

CRESSIDA. Tt tt.

MICHELE. And you still live there, do you?

TERRY. No. I moved away.

Slight pause.

Like so many, both before and doubtless since. From the coal face to the chalk face.

FRANKIE (*whispers, to* MICHELE). *Chalk* face?

MICHELE (*whispers, to* FRANKIE). School.

CRESSIDA. So do you do much with the welfare and the union?

FRANKIE. No, no. I mean, occasionally they have a disco. And from time to time I go up for some bingo with me mam.

CRESSIDA. No, I meant, I don't know, trips, or the colliery brass band, or –

FRANKIE. What, the band? You must be joking.

CRESSIDA. Why?

Pause.

FRANKIE. Well, it's a bit naff, really, isn't it? You know, ta-ra-ra-boomdiay.

MICHELE. To be honest, it's the boys that put you off. All a bit poncy, really.

HOWARD. Poncy?

MICHELE. Yuh, you know, a bit effete.

Pause.

TERRY. Near where I was born, there was a pit, which had a lodge, which had a banner, with the slogan: 'Come, let us reason together'. And I thought that was socialism. Reasoning together. But of course that was in the bad old days. Before the reactionaries and paper tigers had this wonderful idea, that the way to stop the people reasoning together was to give them – rather, sell them – music centres, TV sets and videos, and cram their clubs with booze and bingo rather than old-fashioned stuff like billiards and all those boring books, so instead of doing things together they'd get done apart. (*Slight pause.*) Beg pardon. (*Pause.*)

CRESSIDA. Look, I wonder if the time has come – to unveil our party pieces. To underline the festive spirit of the evening.

HOWARD. What a wonderful idea. So who'll kick off, then?

TERRY. Daniel?

DANIEL. Me?

During the following, there is an increasing amount of nudging and pushing between FRANKIE *and* MICHELE.

CRESSIDA. Why not? Didn't Howard say you learnt to tapdance at some stage?

DANIEL. About a hundred years ago. And I was awful.

HOWARD. They must have taught you something at your nice new school.

DANIEL. You leave my mother out of this.

CRESSIDA. Or perhaps we should start off with Terry's folk song.

DANIEL. Folk song?

TERRY. P'raps a little later.

HOWARD. He needs to, like, crank up a bit. Get the old foot stomping. Screw the finger in the ear.

TERRY. My repertoire is drawn from the industrial tradition. We stick our fingers somewhere altogether different.

HOWARD. How quaint.

CRESSIDA. Look, do I detect some pressure being put on here?

FRANKIE *and* MICHELE *realise the attention is on them.*

FRANKIE. Oh, no.

MICHELE. No. Definitely not.

Slight pause.

HOWARD (*carefully*). Of course the point of opening is that once you've done it you can sit back and get pissed and heckle everybody else. Well, that's always seemed the point to me.

CRESSIDA. The principle that one should remain slightly less drunk than one's audience.

HOWARD. Exactly so.

The girls are weakening. TERRY *leans over.*

TERRY. Go on. You show me yours, I'll show you mine.

The girls look at each other. In exaggerated pantomime, they

begin to suck their lips and shake their heads. But then,
suddenly, MICHELE *turns back to the company.*

MICHELE. Right then. You're on.

CRESSIDA. That's *wonderful.*

FRANKIE (*checking the running order*). Krrk. Working miners?

MICHELE. Krrk krrk. Margaret Thatcher, working miners, Ian
McGregor —

FRANKIE. Krrk krrk Kinnock?

HOWARD. What's with 'krrk krrk'?

TERRY. As in Delta Foxtrot.

And we realise the girls have been imitating the little
noise on policeman's walkie-talkies.

MICHELE. Krrk krrk, Kinnock *then* McGregor.

FRANKIE. Wilcoe.

MICHELE. Right.

MICHELE *stands on her chair, followed by* FRANKIE.

We did this at a talent contest, see. Fund-raiser.

CRESSIDA. That's a nice idea.

FRANKIE. What? It was terrible. Really embarrassing.

TERRY. Did you win then?

MICHELE *looks witheringly at* TERRY.

MICHELE. One, two, three.

The girls sing:

MICHELE *and* FRANKIE.
What shall we do with Margaret Thatcher
What shall we do with Margaret Thatcher
What shall we do with Margaret Thatcher
Early in the morning

Cut her down to size and privatise her
Cut her down to size and privatise her
Cut her down to size and privatise her
Early in the morning

The song continues on the same principle. Everyone except
HOWARD *is drawn into the choruses.*

FRANKIE. ⎫
MICHELE. ⎭   What shall we do with

FRANKIE. ⎫   Neil —
MICHELE. ⎭   Working —

FRANKIE. ⎫   — miners?
MICHELE. ⎭   Sling 'em to the bottom of the nearest pitshaft

What shall we do with Neil Kinnock
Stick him in the flightpath of a flying picket

What shall we do with Ian McGregor?
Hang hang hang the bastard

And, finally:

Burn burn burn the bastards
Burn burn burn the bastards
Burn burn burn the bastards
Early in the morning!

They finish. Enthusiastic applause from TERRY *and*
CRESSIDA, *slightly mocking clapping from* DANIEL.
HOWARD *doesn't applaud, but gets up and goes to get
another bottle of wine, which he brings to the table with a
corkscrew as*:

CRESSIDA. Wonderful.

TERRY. You woz robbed.

CRESSIDA. Well, certainly, the opposition must have been
terrifically impressive.

TERRY. I'd demand a recount.

HOWARD *pointedly opening the wine.*

CRESSIDA. Howard, is there something wrong?

HOWARD. Well, no, not really. It's just, as it happens, I don't
believe in burning Neil Kinnock. He's the leader of the party I
vote for. Nor, actually, do I believe in dropping working
miners down pitshafts, or even hanging Ian McGregor.

The girls don't know how to react.

In fact, I think it's exactly what's wrong with the way this strike's being conducted. Mindless, malicious and macho.

Pause.

CRESSIDA. Howard, it's only —

HOWARD. And I think it would be actually rather condescending, I mean, it would be patronising, just to — clap politely, and say, dears, well that was very nice, now can we change the subject please.

He puts down the corkscrew and sits. CRESSIDA *stands and goes out.* TERRY, *quietly, speaks a verse of the Blackleg Miner*:

TERRY. 'O don't you gan near the Seghill mine
    For across the way they'll hang a line
    To catch the throat and break the spine
    Of the dirty blackleg miner'.

HOWARD. You what?

TERRY. But I suppose that's okay 'cos it's *old.*

HOWARD. No. No, now you come to mention it, I don't agree. I think there is a tendency to sentimentalise the past. In fact, I'm not at all convinced by this idea of yours that it was all Sibelius and quiet evenings boning up on William Morris in t'lodge library, before everybody got brutalised by electronic amplification, Dallas and Keg bitter. I imagine, actually, that an aggressive, tribal and, might we say, machismo culture was just as prevalent in 1926 as 1984.

TERRY. Oh, sure. So how —

Enter CRESSIDA. *She has a book, a pad of paper and a pencil.*

HOWARD. I mean, how do you *really* think they're reacting to the women, in the villages? To their wives going off to London, Brussels and Turin, addressing meetings, leaving them to mind the kids and cook the tea? I mean, Frankie, what do you think that Alun *really* feels about all that?

To FRANKIE's *relief,* CRESSIDA *interrupts.*

CRESSIDA. Over four thousand years ago, when the First Emperor Fu Hsi ruled all things under heaven, he saw the bright patterns of the sky, the shapes of the earth, the distinctive markings in the beasts and birds and living things. And from these configurations he divined eight sacred trigrams, from which it is possible to deduce the character of everything, which is not chicken soup, but does go a long way to explain the hidden workings of the universe.

TERRY. What's this?

HOWARD. Chris, do you take that everywhere?

CRESSIDA. It never leaves my side.

CRESSIDA *sits, opens the book — which is the 'I Ching' — and continues to speak.*

For from those trigrams did arise this book, the I Ching, oracle of change, containing no less than sixty-four configurations, in the form of hexagrams, in which the ancient forces, yin and yang, the passive and the active, feminine and masculine . . .

HOWARD. Aha.

CRESSIDA. . . . are set in constant flux and conflict one with t'other, and through which he or she who would confront the aforesaid hidden wisdoms of the universe may by the throwing of three coins six times reveal the mysteries of what is yet to be. So. Anybody want a go? (*Pause.*) Say — Howard's trip? Or Daniel's prospects? Will Michele dig up the site of Camelot? (*Pause.*) Howard. Why don't you kick off, show 'em how it's done.

HOWARD, *against his better judgement, starts tossing coins,* CRESSIDA *noting down the results.*

Ah. Yang. (*To the young people.*) You see, I'm rather younger than these folks. When I went up to university, the 60s had already gone occult. So at the stage when Howard was immersed in Mao Tse Tung and Che Guevara . . .

TERRY. . . . obviously not *too* thoroughly . . .

CRESSIDA. . . . I was into Nostradamus, motorcycle

maintenance and sacrificing virgins.

TERRY (*to* MICHELE). Sorry, chuck. That is unless —

MICHELE. Tt — nice!

Now CRESSIDA *is looking up* HOWARD's *hexagram — the 14th — in the sacred book.*

CRESSIDA. Right, then.

DANIEL. So, is Seb Coe going to win the 1500?

CRESSIDA. Daniel, you don't play hoot'n'nanny on a Strad. (*Reading the result*:) Howard, I'm pleased to tell you that your trip will be crowned with progress and success. If you spurn that which is harmful, and avoid all error, you will achieve considerable prosperity. You may even end up crossing the great water, but on that I wouldn't bet. Who's next? (*To* FRANKIE *and* MICHELE:) So. One of you?

The GIRLS *don't look enthusiastic.* CRESSIDA *passes the coins to* TERRY.

Our Terry?

TERRY *passes the coins to the* GIRLS.

TERRY (*pointedly, directed at* HOWARD). Encore.

Slight pause.

FRANKIE (*with a shrug*). OK, then. If you like like.

CRESSIDA. Just throw the coins.

FRANKIE *tosses the coins.*

FRANKIE. What's that mean?

CRESSIDA. Nothing yet. One heads, two tails, that's Yin. Go on, again.

As CRESSIDA *notes the first line,* FRANKIE *throws again.*

Yang. Once again. Six times.

FRANKIE *carries on throwing the coins, as:*

MICHELE. So where you going, Howard?

HOWARD. I've got to go and see these television people.

FRANKIE (*as she tosses*). What, on your holidays?

CRESSIDA. It's a mystery how far these people push their luck.

DANIEL. Why, aren't they paying him?

HOWARD. Yes, they are paying him.

CRESSIDA. So they may have got his body, but can they buy his soul? Right, Frankie, what d'you want to know?

FRANKIE (*tosses for the last time*). Like what?

CRESSIDA (*looking through the book*). Well, anything you want to know about yourself.

FRANKIE. What, like me inside leg?

CRESSIDA. No, it's not a quiz. It's about what's going to happen in your future life. What the future holds for you.

MICHELE *flashes a look to* FRANKIE. *Pause.*

FRANKIE. Okay. What's going to happen in my life? What does the future hold for me?

There is a careless, almost sarcastic tone in FRANKIE's *speech that worries* HOWARD. CRESSIDA *finds the commentary on the 32nd hexagram.*

CRESSIDA (*from the oracle*). All right. The answer lies in the hexagram called Heng, which means 'Of Long Duration'. Its trigrams, Chen and Sun, mean thunder, and a gentle wind. Its meaning is that the earth endows all things, and through the seasons constantly renews itself. The lower trigram warns you that you must not dwell on sacrifice, however painful and however hard it may be to endure, but rather on the promise of good fortune, and the certainty that like the seasons winter will give way to spring. Whereas, the upper trigram —

FRANKIE *stands quickly and runs apart, bursting into tears.* MICHELE *follows quickly.*

Oh, crumbs, I'm sorry —

MICHELE. Now come on, Frankie, it's —

CRESSIDA. What a silly *fool* —

CRESSIDA *and* HOWARD *go over to* FRANKIE
and MICHELE.

MICHELE. Now just try and calm down, now . . .

TERRY (*to* HOWARD *and* CRESSIDA). Just let — just let
Michele —

MICHELE. Now try and think about some nice thing, eh? Think
about Norman.

MICHELE *turns to the adults to explain her strategy.*

She's got a cat called Norman. Don't ask me why. (*To*
FRANKIE.) And about your holiday in Yugoslavia. You
enjoyed that, right? And d'you remember that, that weird
boy, what was his name? Mihallo?

FRANKIE. No, Mihailo.

MICHELE. What?

FRANKIE. Mihailo. And he wasn't weird. Well, not really.

MICHELE (*to* HOWARD). You see, she had this holiday last
year.

FRANKIE'*s recovering.*

(*To* FRANKIE.) Now, just think about Mihailo. And you'll be
all right. (*To* CRESSIDA.) You see, I'm trying to keep her mind
off things'll make her cry. Like the strike. The future. Stuff like
that. (*To* FRANKIE.) Now, shall we go back to the table? Or
d'you want to go off to the room, just for a little while?

FRANKIE. Perhaps. The room.

MICHELE. Okay.

She helps FRANKIE *to go.*

And p'raps, while you're out there, it might be best if I
explained why you're upset.

FRANKIE *looks at* MICHELE.

I think that would be best, you know.

Pause. Then FRANKIE *bursts into tears and runs out.*

FRANKIE. Say what you like!

MICHELE *is making to follow when* HOWARD *stops her.*

HOWARD. Look, Michele, I think there's something that I ought to say.

TERRY. Um, are you sure – ?

HOWARD. Yes. Absolutely sure. Because I think – that Frankie ought to know, that it's all right.

MICHELE. I'm sorry.

HOWARD. She's not pregnant.

MICHELE. Pregnant?

HOWARD. That test. In the pantry. It was negative. So if it's that that was upsetting her . . .

MICHELE. What? Frankie? Thought that she was pregnant?

Pause.

HOWARD. Yes?

MICHELE (*a little offended*). I'm sorry, no. I mean we're friends you see. I'd know that. No, it's nothing of that character, I can assure you.

HOWARD *turns to* CRESSIDA.

HOWARD. Then –

MICHELE. No, it's very simple, really. Like, Frankie used to skate.

TERRY. What, roller-skate?

MICHELE. No, ice-skate. Figure skating. And she was supposed to be, like for her age, well, really ace. Not international level, mind, but if she took it seriously, and got the practice and the ice-time, and the tutoring and stuff like that, I'm not quite sure how it works, like, but there's various levels, and if she really worked at it, and went to stay at Swansea with her gran, like in the holidays, so as she could use the rink, they said she could have got her grades for national competition. And then, like, she'd not be Jane Torvill, but . . . who knows? (*Pause.*) She got the skates for Christmas. You know, the proper standard, all that stuff. But when it was obvious the strike was going to last, she sold 'em back. And gave her mum and dad the cash, you see. (*Pause.*) And she doesn't mind. To be honest, she was really pleased that she could make a sacrifice. But just, there's moments, like when you asked her about tennis lessons, or like when the conversation turns to stuff like what's the future, she does get a bit upset. That's all.

FRANKIE *has re-entered.*

FRANKIE. You told 'em.

MICHELE. Yes.

FRANKIE (*to the others*). I'm sorry.

CRESSIDA. No. No, it's us that should be sorry. Me.

FRANKIE. It's just, you see . . . I know we must look very backward to you, very immature . . .

CRESSIDA. Oh, no —

FRANKIE. . . . Well, if we do, it's right, we are, I mean, we don't get half of what you're saying, let's be honest, specially when you're being clever about reactionaries and running dogs, we don't know half the time you're being serious, and like when you ask us things, about ourselves, we're just praying it's a question we can answer. Or if it isn't, we can make it up. (*Pause.*) Like, we talk about what we might have to say. (*Pause.*) Like, Michele isn't really going to be an archaeologist. She made it up. Spur of the moment, you could say. (*Pause.*) 'Cos, to be honest, kind of future that you think about, the kind of future that's a normal thing for you . . . for us, it's just a joke. I mean, like just a fantasy.

Pause.

HOWARD. I think — I think perhaps —

MICHELE. Say what you said.

FRANKIE. Say what?

MICHELE. Say what you said, about her being like a skater.

FRANKIE. Oh —

MICHELE. Just tell 'em what you said.

Pause. FRANKIE *looks to the others, finally to* TERRY.

TERRY. Go on.

FRANKIE. Well, all I said was. That you know they call her 'iron maiden'. But I don't see her in that light at all. (*Pause.*) Like, I see her like those posh girls at the rink in Swansea, gliding so easy 'cross the ice, like they haven't got a care. 'Cos you see, I think, to her, we're only frozen faces. Faces, frozen in the ice, for her to glide upon. I think she skates on people's faces. (*Pause.*) And let's be frank. However much you care, you're the spectators. You are looking on. While we — we're looking up.

Long pause.

HOWARD. Look. Look. (*Pause.*) Look, Frankie, we —

CRESSIDA. Howard, you and I have got to have a conversation.

Blackout.

ACT TWO

Scene One

Sunday 12 August 1984. In the living room, HOWARD *lies asleep on a chair in front of* TERRY's *television. He is dressed informally, but for town. He has dropped off in front of last night's Olympic track and field finals. Now the breakfast programme is recapping the night's events in other sports.* CRESSIDA *enters from the interior of the house, in her nightclothes, carrying a cup of coffee and a magazine, which she intends to take on to the terrace. She sees* HOWARD. *She breathes a little, then goes over, stands in front of him. He wakes. She holds the coffee out to him.*

CRESSIDA. Archery?

    HOWARD *takes the cup and drinks.*

HOWARD. I was eager not to miss the coxless fours.

CRESSIDA. How did Seb do?

    HOWARD *imitates the miler Sebastian Coe's victory gesture.*

    Well, that's good news for all us oldies. Howard, why —

HOWARD. I decided to come back.

CRESSIDA. I wasn't sure if you'd decided that you'd gone.

HOWARD. I meant, earlier than planned. (*Pause.*) No more was I.

CRESSIDA. I'm not — if it's of interest, I don't think I'm pregnant.

HOWARD. Ah. (*Pause.*) This from your apparatus in the pantry?

CRESSIDA. No. I sought professional advice.

HOWARD. That's fast. I thought you had to send off entrails to the hospital.

CRESSIDA. Your friendly local pharmacist will cope.

HOWARD. What, Jones the Truss?

CRESSIDA. More Jones the knowing little wink. He says it's 95 per cent, but it's a little early to be absolutely sure. So if nothing happens by tomorrow, I'll send off another sample to old Doc McWhatsisname.

HOWARD. What, in the post?

CRESSIDA. Mr Jones has an assistant. They're a chatty pair. There is something uniquely demeaning about listening to a long discussion of one's piss in Welsh.

Slight pause.

HOWARD. Did he have a view as to why you're nine days late?

CRESSIDA. Well, the usual diagnosis is some kind of psycho-, some emotional upheaval, isn't it? Either that or a very early menopause.

HOWARD. Now, in what sense could we say that you've been emotionally upheaved?

She senses he wants her to repeat it.

CRESSIDA. Howard. I've just had a love affair.

Pause.

HOWARD. You mean the one with, whatsit?

CRESSIDA. Derek. Yes, of course. (*Slight pause.*) As opposed to what?

HOWARD. Well, all I thought was, all I wondered was if you had got involved with all of this, the strike, because you wanted an affair —

CRESSIDA. What, only in it for the fellas? Howard —

HOWARD. Or whether, rather, the affair came out of what you found inside yourself. Through your involvement with the strike. (*Pause.*) Or rather, even ratherer, what you found within yourself, through it, that you had lost, or never had, with us.

Pause.

CRESSIDA. Point taken.

HOWARD. What if they lose?

CRESSIDA. They won't.

HOWARD. Why not?

CRESSIDA. They can't.

HOWARD. How do you see them winning?

CRESSIDA. Winter. Power cuts. That's how they'll win.

HOWARD. There's a third of them at work.

CRESSIDA. Why don't you want them to?

Pause.

HOWARD. That isn't fair.

CRESSIDA. Oh, isn't it?

Pause.

HOWARD. How could it be?

CRESSIDA. I just, you see, just wonder, with you old 68-ers, if you hadn't got things really rather nicely sorted, with your realignments, new configurations, forward march of labour halted, gourmet socialism, all that stuff. And that, therefore, that all this, and these, these wonderful brave people in their T-shirts and their trainers, up against the helmets and the truncheons and the shields − a bit unwelcome. Uninvited. Tapping at the window. Spectres at the feast. You know?

HOWARD. Oh, yes. I know. I know it well. Indeed, you could say it's something of a *deja vu.*

Pause.

For nearly 4,000 years ago, when even I was young, the prevailing view was very much the same. The proletariat eliminated from the van of history. The workers bought off and sucked in. But then came Edward Heath, and all those dock and rail and coal strikes, and we all thought: hey, perhaps the working class's revolutionary demise has been, well, just a mite exaggerated. Until it became, well, equally transparent that what had actually been exaggerated was their resurrection. That however much we might regret it, we'd been dead right all along. And however much *I* might, and do, regret it now −

CRESSIDA *interrupts. Simply*:

CRESSIDA. Knock knock. Who's there?

HOWARD. Well, even so. And don't — don't feel too good about it. Don't fall into that trap. Because, in fact, it's relatively easy — I mean, in the same way as it's relatively easy to have a nice-and-comfortable, no-ties-on-either-side —

CRESSIDA. Oh, Howard —

HOWARD. — in the same way, it is actually not hard, *that* hard, to run a strike in summertime, in your T-shirts and your trainers. But what happens in the winter, Chris? When it's not that they can't have ice creams, but the parcels have dried up and they're down to baked beans every night and they've outgrown all their shoes?

CRESSIDA. Howard, it will be over —

HOWARD. What, 'by Christmas'?

CRESSIDA. Yes. By Christmas, certainly. All will be crowned with great victory and success.

HOWARD. But if it isn't, Cressida?

Pause.

CRESSIDA. You sound like Gillian.

HOWARD. I don't. She'd say —

CRESSIDA. No, I meant the mode of discourse.

HOWARD. *She*'d say, that if she can overcome those centuries of patriarchy, if she'd cracked PMT, if she'd made it in the world against the odds, why on earth can't everybody else. Your pit's closed? Simple. Why not start up a little graphics firm in Camden Town. That's what Gillian would say.

CRESSIDA. Yes. Yes, she did.

HOWARD. Did? When?

CRESSIDA. Last night. She rang.

HOWARD. Rang? Why?

CRESSIDA. 'Cos Danny had rung her.

HOWARD. Dan- Why? Whatever for?

CRESSIDA. To ask her if she'd come and take him home.

Pause.

HOWARD. I see.

CRESSIDA. There's been, well, some emotion since you left.

HOWARD. That's 'since'?

CRESSIDA. Okay, as well. The girls were mortified about that stuff on Thursday night, kept going on about how awful it had been, to have to make an exhibition of themselves, in front of us.

HOWARD. You did assure them that we are *quite* as capable of making —

CRESSIDA. 'Us' in the sense of, middle-class people.

HOWARD. Christ.

CRESSIDA. Overhearing which, Daniel said just what you've said, borrowed 10p and jogged straight off to the payphone.

HOWARD. I'm not sure I can take this before breakfast.

CRESSIDA. I'm not sure I can take it before coffee.

HOWARD *realises* CRESSIDA *gave him her coffee.*

HOWARD. Hey, let me —

CRESSIDA. No, I . . . (*Pause.*) It's in the cafetière.

HOWARD *makes to go, then turns back.*

HOWARD. Chris. It isn't, honestly. It isn't the affair. It is this.

CRESSIDA. You mean —

HOWARD. I mean, I've noticed how it's changed you. How you dazzle, how you're like a child in a new house, you're running round and flinging open all the doors and windows, letting in the light, and shouting, crikey, look what's here. (*Pause.*) Whereas, for me . . . I've seen the sights before. If not the same, then desperately similar. There is no novel feature, no surprise. (*Pause.*) But I don't want *you* to see it like that, Cressida. I want you to look with wonder. And I worry that

I block your light. That I draw the curtains, close the shutters, shut the door. And that — that isn't fair.

Pause.

CRESSIDA. I was last here when I was ten. In Daniel's position, in reverse. And he was wonderful, my new dad, he was great. He taught me everything. The rocks, the tides, the seaweed, the crustacea. He opened up the wonders of the world. (*Pause.*) Look, all I wanted — 'cos I knew I wouldn't get you touting outside Budgens, but I wanted you to get involved. That's why I said that we could take a kid, or kids. Because I wanted you to get involved. I wanted to see you be right again. I thought that you'd have things to say. That you'd have, wisdom, to pass on. (*Pause.*) He gave me the most dazzling of summers. But however wonderful it is, to be at someone's knee, there comes a point, you have to stand up and confront them face to face.

Pause.

HOWARD. Are you disappointed?

CRESSIDA. What about?

HOWARD. Your news.

A very slight pause.

CRESSIDA. Why should I be?

Pause.

HOWARD. I'll get your coffee, Cressida.

HOWARD *goes out.* CRESSIDA *isn't sure what's happened. Absently, she turns up the TV volume. We hear what is obviously the re-showing of the last lap of the 1500 metres final.* CRESSIDA *turns off the television and goes on to the terrace.* HOWARD *enters, quickly, with* CRESSIDA's *coffee.*

HOWARD. Chris, has the reformation of the working class spread to the girls?

CRESSIDA. What do you mean?

HOWARD. Have they mutated into early risers?

CRESSIDA. Goodness, no.

HOWARD. They've gone.

CRESSIDA. You what?

HOWARD. They've risen. They're not here.

CRESSIDA. Oh, cripes. You're sure?

HOWARD. Of course.

CRESSIDA. Oh gosh, what are we going to say —

> HOWARD, *who's facing towards the beach, suddenly laughs.*
>
> Howard, this isn't *funny.*

HOWARD. No, it's Frankie. Coming from the beach.

CRESSIDA. The beach?

HOWARD. Hey, you don't suppose they've actually swum?

CRESSIDA. Howard, she is carrying a beach towel.

HOWARD. Stranger things have happened.

CRESSIDA. Kind of, splattered —

HOWARD. Do we — ?

CRESSIDA. We do now.

> *They look at each other, and then start to move just as*
> FRANKIE *runs on to the terrace, in her bathing suit,*
> *carrying a white beach towel splattered with blood.*

FRANKIE. Michele.

CRESSIDA. What's happened?

FRANKIE. Uh — Michele. With Terry.

HOWARD. Terry?

FRANKIE. Blood — blood everywhere.

CRESSIDA. Oh, crumbs —

FRANKIE. Huge gash. Blood everywhere.

> *Enter* TERRY *supporting* MICHELE, *who is indeed bleeding*
> *substantially from her foot. They are both in bathing*
> *costumes.* MICHELE *wears a sunhat.*

TERRY. Our early swim. A triumph of logistics, not to say persuasion. Sadly, at the crucial moment, Michele slipped and cut her foot.

CRESSIDA. Are you — is she —

TERRY. We are being very brave. Do we have some TCP?

TERRY is helping MICHELE on to the recliner.

CRESSIDA. Sure do.

CRESSIDA goes out through the house. MICHELE lies back on the recliner, takes off her hat.

HOWARD. What did she cut it on?

TERRY. Well, we don't think it was broken glass or a tin or anything. But it's better to be sure.

HOWARD. Yes. Right.

TERRY. Now, are you feeling faint at all, Michele?

MICHELE. No. No.

Re-enter CRESSIDA with TCP, a clean towel, bandages, cotton wool and a bowl.

CRESSIDA. Right. Here we are.

TERRY. Thank goodness for the guides.

CRESSIDA. Now you can stop all that. Is there anything else that you require?

TERRY. Uh — breakfast? If —

CRESSIDA. Dib dib.

She's going out.

HOWARD. I'll help.

HOWARD follows. TERRY sits down to bathe and bandage MICHELE's foot. FRANKIE stands, agitating.

FRANKIE. Terry. Will she —

TERRY (*pointedly*). I'm convinced she'll walk again.

MICHELE. Why's Howard back so early?

TERRY. Of that I'm less sure. Why doesn't Frankie go and ask him?

FRANKIE. I'm going sunbathing. Let her get gangrene. See if I care.

FRANKIE *goes out round the side of the house.*

MICHELE. Always a fusser, Frankie.

TERRY. Mm. You should have worn something on your feet.

MICHELE. Well, I would have done. Only Frankie couldn't find her trainers.

TERRY. Sorry?

MICHELE. So I said, okay, I won't wear mine.

TERRY. Um — I'm not sure —

MICHELE. See, if I'd worn mine, and Frankie didn't have hers, she'd have an excuse, like, wouldn't she? So I says, I'll go barefoot, and we're equal, like, and so she don't have no excuse.

TERRY. I see. (*Pause.*) You didn't have to come.

MICHELE. Oh, no, I wanted to. But, see, we wanted to feel easier about the situation here, before consigning our young bodies to the waves. I mean, you know what teenage girls are like.

TERRY *is rather thrown by this.*

TERRY. Well, in a broad —

MICHELE. And particularly, having made such idiots of ourselves the other night.

TERRY. You didn't.

MICHELE. Yes, we did.

TERRY. You wouldn't have thought twice about it, if they'd been your class.

MICHELE. No. But they aren't.

Pause.

TERRY. What did they say? Your mum and dad?

MICHELE. Oh, best behaviour. Emissaries of the strike. Ambassadors for our community.

TERRY. And did you like that? Was that a role you enjoy?

MICHELE *doesn't answer.*

Tell me what you find most strange.

MICHELE. Fellow called Terry.

TERRY. Seriously.

MICHELE. Salad bowls.

TERRY. Beg pardon?

MICHELE. Having food served separate. Salad and vegetables and all that stuff. Like, you've no idea how much you're s'posed to take.

TERRY. And anything annoy you? Or upset you?

Pause.

MICHELE. Not so much 'annoy'.

TERRY. Go on.

MICHELE. It's just . . . It's easy to − be sentimental, if you follow me. The morning mist. The lowering slate-grey sky. The 30s, and the General Strike and stuff like that. You forget, you all know more 'bout that than we do. And of course, it's got its features. Friendliness. Like, everybody caring for each other. Walk along the street, know everybody, say hello. But it can be − restricted. Rather tight. If you don't fit. I mean, there's people who can't wait to go. (*Slight pause.*) I mean, I know I did wrong, making jokes 'bout being queer, and stuff like that. But, a bloke being queer in a mining village, to be honest, he'd not last five minutes. Really.

TERRY. No. I didn't.

Pause.

MICHELE. Pardon?

TERRY. Didn't last five minutes. Really.

MICHELE *can't speak.*

TERRY. When were you born?

MICHELE. The third of April 1969.

TERRY. Well, when you were, God help us, three, some London
    dockworkers mounted a campaign to save their jobs. And
    eventually six of them were thrown in jail. And there was a
    huge campaign to get them out, which culminated in this
    massive march to Pentonville. The prison, in which they were
    consigned. And I'd been living in, or rather round, a group of
    people in West London of an anarchist persuasion, among
    whom, frankly, being queer was if anything encouraged.
    But, on this march, surrounded by the best, the brightest,
    the most militant and self-assured and conscious and aware of
    all the working class, I had this strange sensation, that I was at
    home. Back home. But for the first time. Ever. Do you see?

MICHELE *nods.*

And I had — we used to wear this little triangle, pink triangle,
a sort of badge, because that's what the homosexuals had had
to wear in the concentration camps in Nazi Germany — you
know, like the Jews wore yellow stars. And my badge was in
my pocket, for I took it, as indeed I take it, everywhere. And
I very nearly put it on. (*Slight pause.*) And last month,
we had a march and rally for the miners. Wonderful. So
wonderful, in fact, so like that time, I very nearly put it on
again.

Pause.

MICHELE. Did they get out? The dockers?

TERRY. Yes, they did.

MICHELE. We thought that you were sweet on Cressida.

TERRY (*with a twinkle*). I am.

MICHELE. No, we meant, like, that — (*She grins, annoyed at
    missing the twinkle.*) Oh, you.

He pats her foot.

TERRY. Right, then.

MICHELE. I'll walk again.

TERRY. You will.

He stands and helps her up.

MICHELE. You know, you should go home. You should tell 'em. Face 'em up to it. It'd do 'em good. My view.

Pause.

TERRY (*ruefully*). Oh you.

FRANKIE *and* CRESSIDA *come round the side of the house.* TERRY *leaves* MICHELE.

CRESSIDA. So, how's the invalid?

TERRY. We may not have to amputate.

CRESSIDA. I'll post a notice.

TERRY. Howard?

CRESSIDA. Bringing stuff in from the car.

TERRY *a questioning look to* CRESSIDA, *as* HOWARD *enters the living room with a big parcel, his overnight bag, and* FRANKIE'*s trainers. He puts the parcel down somewhere inconspicuous and goes on to the terrace.*

He – decided to come back. Now, breakfast, anybody?

HOWARD *appears with the shoes.*

HOWARD. Frankie, I'm sorry. In the boot.

FRANKIE. My trainers.

MICHELE *looks ruefully at her foot.*

TERRY. Did I hear loose talk of breakfast?

CRESSIDA (*pointing round the side*). Thataway.

DANIEL *runs on to the terrace. He bends double and breathes heavily.*

HOWARD. Good morning, Daniel.

TERRY *picks up a note in* HOWARD'*s voice.*

TERRY. Right, then. Hobble on.

TERRY *helps* MICHELE *round the side of the house.*

FRANKIE *takes her trainers in through the house.* DANIEL *unbends.*

CRESSIDA. She cut her foot.

DANIEL. Oh dear. How dreadful. Howard, can I use your shower?

HOWARD. Daniel, why did you call Gillian?

DANIEL *looks at* HOWARD, *then* CRESSIDA.

CRESSIDA. She rang last night.

DANIEL. Why shouldn't I?

HOWARD. No reason. But if you're unhappy here, it would be nice if we knew too.

DANIEL *sits.*

DANIEL. Right, then. Family discussion. Minutes of last meeting. Take as read. Matters arising. None. Apologies for absence. Well —

HOWARD. Daniel, this is ridiculous. You're here for a fortnight —

DANIEL. Item four. Holiday. Position on. Characterisation of. A) A time of respite and amusement, often in association with recreation, tourism and travel; or B) guilt trip.

Pause.

HOWARD. All right, then. Go and have your shower.

CRESSIDA. Howard —

DANIEL (*stands*). I mean, do you have any idea how ridiculous you look? You're so keen not to patronise them for being miners' children, you forget they're teenage girls and treat them like they're 40, middle-class and male. And when you're not doing that, it's stuff like accusing them of being pregnant. And that's when you're not giving Frankie the third degree about the fucking Spanish Civil War.

Pause.

Who knows? Who cares? It's something that's embarrassing, or silly, or — just something that she doesn't much want to discuss. It's not like, some great drama. It's like where they live. Sure, for you, it's 'The Rhondda', clenched fists and stirring music and lodge banners fluttering in the wind. But for them, it's dull and grimy and there aren't any decent shops or discos, and it's — just the fucking boring place they live in. And they want to leave it. Just like Terry, eh?

HOWARD. In fact, I've found out about the Civil War. And it's not embarrassing or silly. It's about her grandad. And the International Brigade.

DANIEL. Well, I'm so pleased for you.

MICHELE *has entered.*

MICHELE. Sorry. Me hat. The sun.

MICHELE *limps over, picks up her hat, and goes back out.*

HOWARD (*shortly*). I'm getting bored with this.

DANIEL (*shortly*). Well, so am I, 'cos I have had it up to here.

Slight pause.

HOWARD. Go on.

DANIEL. With everything. From my stupid name, to not having proper toys. To explaining to my friends why my parents dress like freaks and have cats called things like Stalin. Not to mention suffering the delusion they were dangerous revolutionists . . . Until, at least, *she* saw the light.

He turns to go. Then turns back.

You said it. They're just ordinary girls. I'm going to take my shower now.

He goes out, through the house.

CRESSIDA. I s'pose . . . there is a sense . . .

HOWARD. Boy, is there ever.

HOWARD *goes into the living room.*

CRESSIDA (*calls*). Howard, what's this about the International Brigade?

HOWARD. Well. The meeting wasn't quite as long as I'd anticipated. And although I'd got some shopping, I had time to pop into the British Library. There was one person from their village killed in Spain. His name was Owen. First name, Frank.

CRESSIDA. Granddaughter.

HOWARD. Or grandniece. But it would explain the reticence now, wouldn't it?

CRESSIDA. Well, in a way. How was your meeting?

Pause. HOWARD goes back on the terrace.

HOWARD. Well, frankly, not too dazzling. (*Slight pause.*) The problem is, they'd got it in their minds, quite how I don't know, that it was spies. That every 30s lefty ended up as Burgess or Maclean. That's those who didn't see the light, like Orwell in Catalonia. And it was felt, with great regret, that somewhere between Le Carré's latest and the hype for 1984 . . . the thing had, now, how can we put this Howard, just gone off the boil.

CRESSIDA. What, you mean, it's cancelled?

HOWARD. Not their view, of course. They're still as keen as mustard. But they wouldn't put its chances, now, at more than five per cent.

CRESSIDA. Howard, I'm sorry.

HOWARD. Are you?

CRESSIDA. Yes, of course I am.

Enter FRANKIE, having changed.

FRANKIE. Oh, I'm sorry, I —

CRESSIDA. Don't worry. Things had reached a natural break.

She goes out round the side of the house.
FRANKIE goes into the living room. HOWARD follows, picks up the parcel, makes to go. FRANKIE looks at the parcel.

HOWARD (*gnomically*). Beware of freaks, bearing gifts.

He goes out. FRANKIE *is left there.* MICHELE *appears.*

MICHELE. Krrk krrk. Do you read me Delta Foxtrot?

FRANKIE. Krrk krrk. Yes, I read you Delta One Control.

MICHELE. They got the Spain thing.

FRANKIE. Oh, shit.

MICHELE. But they think it's your grand*dad*.

FRANKIE. Grand*dad*?

MICHELE. That's right. They think he was a soldier in the civil war.

FRANKIE. Oh, well.

Slight pause.

Oh, well, *that*'d be all right. I mean, they'd quite like that, wouldn't they?

MICHELE. Krrk krrk. Why need they ever know?

Blackout.

Scene Two

Early evening. A day or two later. Pimms in a jug and glasses in the living room. On the terrace, two parcels wrapped in gift paper are behind a chair. DANIEL sits, to the side, on the recliner, reading the 'I Ching' and sipping a drink. He is dressed smartly. As the scene develops, he'll find three coins in his pocket and start to cast them to form hexagrams. But this, if not surreptitious, is at least a private activity.
HOWARD and TERRY come on to the terrace. They too are both dressed smartly, for an evening out. Both men have drinks. They are arguing.

HOWARD. I'm sorry, I still don't see the problem.

TERRY. Well, can I count the ways. They'll be embarrassed. They'll feel patronised. They'll see it as an act of charity —

HOWARD. Oh, charity, well I'm *so* sorry —

TERRY. Howard, you know what this strike's all about. They have been scrupulous. I've seen them sharing out the cornflakes. Virtually counting grains of rice. And it is via the rediscovery of those old principles, of equality of suffering, of share and share alike — What do you think?

CRESSIDA has appeared. She's dressed in a heavily patterned, flowing dress, with dramatic earrings.

CRESSIDA. What do I think of what?

HOWARD. Ah, Cressida. An Indian restaurant?

CRESSIDA. I'm sorry?

TERRY. Howard. Just think of it, from her point of view. She makes what is by any definition a great sacrifice. Then you turn round and say it wasn't worth it.

HOWARD. That is an utter travesty —

TERRY. She makes that sacrifice first, I imagine, out of a commitment to her family, then to the industry, and finally her community, a community which is itself reasserting its own historical identity, its sense of solidarity, its consciousness . . .

HOWARD. Well, I'm sorry, I'm not hearing that. I'm hearing something rather different.

TERRY. What's that?

HOWARD. I'm hearing a community that Frankie and Michele want to defend, yes, sure, but also want to leave. And I'm hearing — well, we all heard, a cry of something like despair, from a girl who'd found a talent, who'd found something in herself that might have *helped* her to —

TERRY. Escape? Get up, get out, get going?

HOWARD. And I'm surprised that you aren't hearing that as well. You of all people.

CRESSIDA. Skating on faces.

HOWARD. That was just a metaphor.

TERRY. I'd drop the 'just'.

HOWARD. It is, you know, in fact, a present. From one person to another. Not political, except of course to those who think that everything's political, from toilet roll to Turandot. It is a gift, an act of kindness and affection, given freely by one person, me, to somebody I know. (*Pause.*) Where the hell are they, anyway? Our table's booked for half-past seven.

CRESSIDA. They are getting ready.

MICHELE *and* FRANKIE *enter the living room. They are once again dressed up, but somehow they look more adult than on their first evening.*

They are ready now.

The girls come on the terrace.

You both look lovely.

FRANKIE. Thank you.

HOWARD. Drinks, drinks, drinks.

HOWARD *goes into the living room and pours Pimms into glasses. He puts the full glasses and the jug on to a tray and brings it out.*

MICHELE. We're looking forward to our treat.

FRANKIE. That's right.

MICHELE. Mind, that doesn't mean we haven't liked our dinners here.

FRANKIE. Oh, no. We've liked 'em all.

Pause.

MICHELE. The lobster was particularly toothsome.

HOWARD. It is called Pimms. It's a kind of fruit cup.

TERRY. With a kick.

FRANKIE. Thank you.

They take drinks. He hands a third full glass to CRESSIDA, *puts down the tray, and offers a refill to* TERRY. TERRY *shakes his head.* HOWARD *fills his own glass and puts the jug down.* DANIEL *goes and refills his glass from the jug.*

HOWARD. Right then.

Pause. MICHELE *and* FRANKIE *look at each other.*

It is — tonight is our last night together. And instead of yet more boring old lobster, we're going to sample the delights of Blas-Ar-Cymru in Llanwen.

FRANKIE (*correction*). Cymru.

HOWARD. Indeed. But before we — left, I felt I ought to say — well, not to say so much as to, well, mark, our feelings . . . With a little something to remember this, this time we've spent together, here in Wales.

He picks up the two parcels and hands them to the girls. TERRY *refuses to watch.*

Michele, and Frankie. With our love.

MICHELE. Oh, crumbs.

Pause. CRESSIDA *can't bear it.*

CRESSIDA. Are they supposed to —

HOWARD. Yes. Please open them.

MICHELE *looks at* FRANKIE *and then opens her parcel.* FRANKIE *sits opening hers too — which is more complicated, as it contains items in tissue paper — but stops when* MICHELE *finds a pair of leather-bound books. She opens the first and looks up at* HOWARD.

It's a Victorian edition of the works of Tennyson. It includes the 'Morte d'Arthur' and the 'Idylls of the King'. The Arthur legend.

MICHELE (*with a little grin*). 'The Death of Arthur'.

HOWARD (*sharing*): Arthur the King. (*Pause.*) There are some, I think, rather lovely illustrations.

MICHELE *finds a picture in the book.*

MICHELE. Yes. Yes. Thank you, very much.

HOWARD. Whereas, for Frankie, there's some items with which we are sure she'll cut a figure —

FRANKIE has found a boot and a set of skating blades.

The boots are WIFA. I'm afraid I had to liberate your trainers for the size. There's a set of figure- and free-skating blades. They're M and K. I'm told —

FRANKIE pushes the parcel away, bursts into tears, and runs out, back through the living room, to her room. MICHELE runs after. No one else moves.

DANIEL. Well. That was —

CRESSIDA. Shut up, Daniel.

DANIEL. I'm sorry.

CRESSIDA looks over to DANIEL, a little surprised by his tone. Pause.

TERRY. Howard. I have to tell you that you've just —

HOWARD. You know, you know what *I* find worst, of all the many things that I find worst about our bleak, mean times, what that bloody woman's done to us, is how we've let her — them — rewrite our history. How in this year of all years, we've allowed them to write off our time.

CRESSIDA. Um, Howard —

HOWARD. And it's — of course it's very easy to write off, all the silliness and grandiosity and triviality, the decade that gave us tower blocks and Chinese heroin and nothing else . . .

TERRY. Well, yur, you can —

HOWARD. But in fact, if you sit down and think about it, if you actually add it up, desegregation, ending of the war, bringing down two presidents, nearly smashing the French state, even dear old here . . . Not to mention all those subtle and yet revolutionary changes in the way we spoke and sang and reached out to each other . . . And of course the rising of the women, and perhaps the rising of the planet, in mute screaming protest against all we'd done to them and her . . . But do you know what it was all about? Why it was so good?

Because it started with four blacks in Carolina who refused to leave a lunch-bar. One young man who was the first to burn his draft card. Students, women, blacks, who laid their, their *own* bodies on a most bewildering array of lines — in order to say, no.

He looks at TERRY, *who shrugs.*

A story. The University of Edinburgh. Where I taught social anthropology, from 1966 to '69. The students' union, divided, men and women. A girl I knew, who had got really pissed off with this situation. So, one Saturday, she dolled herself up in what I think is called a cocktail dress, she went down to the men's union, on her own, and entered the great bar — no doubt among the longest in the western world — and strolled up to the counter bold as brass and inquired if they could furnish her with one small g and t. And the barman said, 'I'm sorry, madam, I can't serve you.' And by now, of course, it being Saturday, not only had her presence been observed, and commented upon, indeed, but by now there was a fearful catcalling, and whistling, and stamping in the gallery; and having asked again, and having been refused again, she began the long walk back, towards the door. And you can imagine both the manner and the matter of the catcalling, and what courage, and indeed what perspicuity, for her to turn back, at the door, to look across that sea of bloated, drunken student faces, smile a withering smile, and drop — one — shoulder strap. And turn, and go. (*Pause.*) In 1967. That time, when young Americans were lying down in front of troop trains. Che Guevara fighting his doomed battles in the hills. Mohammed Ali saying, 'Hell no, I won't go.' That time. That summer.

Silence. HOWARD *looks at* FRANKIE'*s parcel. He takes out the other boot and a second set of blades. He looks at them, and sets them down.*

DANIEL. Who was the woman? Was that Cressida?

CRESSIDA. In 1967, dear, I was fifteen. No, I assume that that was Gillian.

HOWARD. That's right. Your mum. In fact, she was actually pregnant at the time. By me. With you.

MICHELE re-enters, alone, through the living room, on to the terrace.

MICHELE. Look.

CRESSIDA. Michele.

MICHELE. Look, Frankie just, just wanted me to tell you, wanted me to say, she's sorry.

HOWARD. Well, she shouldn't be. It was a stupid —

MICHELE. But she was so moved.

Pause.

HOWARD. I'm sorry?

MICHELE. And she just, couldn't speak, you see. She couldn't work out what to say.

Pause.

Because . . . she was so moved. And grateful.

No one can say anything. FRANKIE enters. There is a pause. Then she speaks, slowly and carefully, to the COMPANY.

FRANKIE. I think, if it's okay, I'd like to have my skates now. Take a look at 'em, before we go to dinner. That's, if that's okay.

Pause. MICHELE hands the skates to FRANKIE, and picks up her books.

MICHELE. We'll be ready in five minutes, then. If you don't mind.

She follows FRANKIE out. Pause. DANIEL picks up the 'I Ching' at the hexagram he found earlier in the scene. It is the 54th.

CRESSIDA. I suppose that someone ought to phone —

DANIEL (*reading*). The Hexagram Kuei Mei. The Marriage of the Maiden. Here the great and righteous relationship of heaven and the earth is signified. If heaven and earth were to have no intercourse, they would not grow and flourish as they do. (*Pause.*) Well, that makes sense to me.

He looks at his father.

I didn't know that, about Gillian.

Blackout.

Scene Three

Next day. Around noon. It's hot — when we see them, the residents are dressed in their brightest, summeriest clothes. ALUN stands in the living room, looking around a certain amount of celebratory debris — bottles, glasses, cups, evidence that the party carried on after the restaurant. No people, however.
ALUN goes out on to the terrace, sees the 'I Ching' where DANIEL left it, picks it up and reads. Then he hears voices from the direction of the beach. DANIEL runs on to the terrace.

DANIEL (*turning back, to announce his victory*). I won I won.

ALUN. Congratulations.

DANIEL. Ah. Hullo.

CRESSIDA *runs in with* FRANKIE.

CRESSIDA. Alun, I'm sorry. We've been saying farewell to the beach.

ALUN. Don't worry. I'm a little early.

Enter HOWARD, *followed by* MICHELE, *who is being helped over the last few yards by* TERRY.

HOWARD. Alun. Good morning. Afternoon.

MICHELE. Eh, Dad.

ALUN. Michele, what's wrong with you?

TERRY. She cut her foot. It's really not that —

MICHELE. Had a relapse. Trying to do too much, too early.

TERRY. It's really not that serious.

MICHELE. Well, that's all you know!

ALUN. You've had these on the beach?

FRANKIE (*to* ALUN). Oh, they been treating us like something terrible. Making us run about. I nearly rang the NSPCC.

DANIEL. I'm going to have my shower now.

CRESSIDA. Don't be too long!

DANIEL *runs out.*

ALUN. Right, now you girls, I've got to be in Ponty for a meeting —

FRANKIE. But we got to pack.

ALUN. You better get moving, then.

TERRY. Krrk krrk. Wilco.

FRANKIE *and* MICHELE *go to their bedroom,* TERRY *goes out to the hall.*

CRESSIDA. Now, a coffee?

HOWARD. Or indeed a beer?

ALUN. Well, actually, I brought some fizzy wine. It's in the fridge.

CRESSIDA. How — wonderful.

CRESSIDA *goes out to the kitchen.* HOWARD *and* ALUN *are left alone.* ALUN *is still holding the 'I Ching'.* HOWARD *notices.* ALUN *looks at the cover.*

ALUN. The — Itching?

HOWARD. *I Ching.* It's a sort of — sophisticated fortune-telling aid. It's been a feature of the holiday. You know, one year it's frisbees, then its boules, this year it's oriental mysticism.

TERRY *takes the cases from the hall across into the rest of the house.*

What's it say?

ALUN. That 'heaven looks on earthly marriage with great favour, but only where the rightful order is observed. Where the weak become superior to the strong, misfortune will result. The young woman bears an empty basket, there is no advantage.'

HOWARD. Some you win and some you lose.

ALUN hands the 'I Ching' to HOWARD, who looks at the passage ALUN has read out as CRESSIDA brings in the wine and glasses.

CRESSIDA. This isn't fizzy wine. This is sparkling Saumur, *méthode champenoise.*

ALUN. Well, I meant, it isn't real champagne.

CRESSIDA. Real schmeal. (*Opening the bottle.*) Right, here we go — here we go —

It pops, as TERRY joins them. HOWARD puts down the oracle.

HOWARD. Ah, Terry. A little something?

TERRY. Just this once.

They have drinks.

ALUN. So, then:

HOWARD. To the mass defection of the intellectual classes to the cause.

CRESSIDA. To the continued moral vulnerability of the shoppers of North Oxford.

TERRY. To a General Strike.

ALUN. Your health.

They drink.

TERRY. So how was Heysham?

ALUN. Power station?

TERRY. Yuh.

ALUN. Oh, fine.

CRESSIDA. You closed it?

ALUN. Well, no, we didn't — being nuclear, we didn't expect that, but we did, we made our point.

HOWARD. That's good.

ALUN. In fact, to be honest, it was something of an experience.

TERRY. In what way?

ALUN. Well, what happened was —

Suddenly, MICHELE *and* FRANKIE *burst into the living room with their cases. They've changed.* MICHELE *has a carrier-bag.*

TERRY. Be-hold.

TERRY, ALUN, HOWARD *and* CRESSIDA *go into the living room. The girls are breathless.*

MICHELE. The landspeed packing record.

ALUN. Beg your pardon?

MICHELE. Smashed.

CRESSIDA. Well, *that* calls for two more glasses.

HOWARD *gets glasses. As he does so:*

HOWARD. In fact, of course, you'd be most welcome, if you'd care to stay for lunch —

CRESSIDA. Howard, (a) Alun's said he's in a hurry, and (b) we've really only just had breakfast.

HOWARD *pours wine. Enter* DANIEL *from his shower.*

HOWARD. Ah, yes. Frankie's amazing eggs.

CRESSIDA. For which we want the recipe before you go. Now, Daniel, wine?

DANIEL. Yes, please.

HOWARD *pours* DANIEL *wine, as :*

TERRY. Well, one says eggs, but there's onions, bacon, peppers red and green —

ALUN. Ah, now, I know where all that comes from. Frankie's Spanish nan.

Pause.

CRESSIDA. Her Spanish nan?

ALUN. That's right. Why, didn't she —

HOWARD. Her Spanish grandmother?

Pause. ALUN *looks at* MICHELE *and* FRANKIE.

FRANKIE. Well . . . It isn't, like, a terrific mystery. It's just that, in the Spanish war, they sent these kids from the Basque provinces to Britain. You know, like as refugees. And there was three homes in Wales. And almost all of them went back, you know, after the war, but one or two, like if they were orphaned or whatever, they stayed on. Got married. So my nan's name is Francesca Williams. (*Slight pause.*) Lives in Swansea. Near the rink.

CRESSIDA. Why didn't you —

HOWARD. Why did they come, the children.

FRANKIE. 'Cos they lost their homes.

HOWARD. Where did they come from?

FRANKIE. Told you. The Basque provinces.

HOWARD. Which town?

Pause.

FRANKIE. Well, several, as I understand —

HOWARD. Yuh, sure. Your nan. Bilbao? Or the other one?

Long pause.

FRANKIE. She still — she says she still can't hear aeroplanes. Still makes her terrified. To look up, see an aeroplane.

Pause.

HOWARD. Frankie. For heaven's sake. Why didn't you tell us that your nan in Swansea came to Wales from Guernica?

TERRY. *Guernica?*

Slight pause.

CRESSIDA. The bombs? Picasso's screaming horses?

HOWARD. That's the one.

Pause.

ALUN. Good question.

DANIEL. Easy answer.

CRESSIDA (*warning*). Daniel —

DANIEL. Well, it's obvious. You want them all to be like heroes. 'A chapter from your glorious history'. That fits, with a grandad dying in a hail of bullets, head held high. Not so good with a frightened, snivelling little girl, with just the clothes she stands up in, who cries and hides each time she hears a plane. Not so good, with someone thrown on others' mercy. With a refugee.

The adults look at the girls. FRANKIE shrugs.

MICHELE. I mean, I didn't know. Ridiculous. I didn't know why Frankie's nan was called Francesca. And had a kind of funny accent. Before it came up on this holiday, I never thought to ask.

Pause.

ALUN. Ah, well. There's been a lot of digging. Lot of stuff we'd let get buried. High time it got dug up. (*Slight pause. He drains his glass.*) Well, now, perhaps the time has come —

MICHELE. Well, no, not quite.

ALUN. Beg pardon?

MICHELE *picks up the carrier. To* ALUN:

MICHELE. See, we had a little present session yesterday, but it all got out of hand. So we didn't give out ours.

HOWARD. Oh, for heaven's sake —

CRESSIDA. Well, goodness.

FRANKIE. It's not much, only strike stuff really. There's a cassette of mining songs, for Terry . . .

The girls hand out the presents.

MICHELE. And a pit lamp key-ring, that's for Howard.

FRANKIE. And a Women Against Pit Closures teatowel, that's for Cressida . . .

MICHELE. . . . or you could swap 'em round —

FRANKIE. And there's a Rhondda mug for Daniel.

MICHELE. So he'll remember how to say it, like.

FRANKIE. And everybody gets a badge.

MICHELE. That is, except for Terry.

Pause.

TERRY. Sorry?

MICHELE. Terry doesn't get a badge.

TERRY. And why not, pray?

MICHELE. 'Less we get a badge from him.

Pause.

FRANKIE. That is a definite decision.

MICHELE. For we know he takes it everywhere. (*Pause.*) 'Cos if you show 'em ours, it's only fair, it's only right we show 'em yours.

After a moment, TERRY *feels in his pocket, and takes out a pink triangle badge. He gives it to* MICHELE, *who looks at it in her hand. Then she speaks to the* COMPANY. *But she can't yet look at her* FATHER.

MICHELE. You see, the way we look at it, is it's not as if you knew us. Not as if we're family or somebody you know. You asked us here as strangers. You accepted us, because our families are suffering. 'Course, you know us *now.* But when you said you'd help us, we were strangers.

Pause.

And it's not just — hospitality. You taught us things about our lives. What's wrong with, you know, with our attitudes. The way we've been brought up, like. Like, the way we are.

CRESSIDA. Oh, no.

HOWARD. No, really not.

MICHELE. Oh, yes. Oh, yes.

Pause.

Oh, yes, there's lots of things, that you passed on to us.

She pins the badge on to herself.

Yes, there's no doubt about it, in my view.

Pause. At last, she looks at ALUN.

ALUN. Um, that's — the gay thing, isn't it?

MICHELE. That's right.

ALUN *turns to* TERRY.

TERRY (*pause*). Oh, yes. (*Pause.*) 'Fraid so.

FRANKIE (*brightly*). Okay. We're ready.

HOWARD. Hey, you didn't tell us about Heysham.

MICHELE. And that recipe —

FRANKIE. Oh, Christ —

CRESSIDA. No. No, I think you should just go.

HOWARD *looks to* CRESSIDA.

And of course we'll see you again soon, and yes, we'll write, and phone, and indeed we want the recipe for Frankie's Spanish eggs, but at this, at this moment, I do think it's best — if you just go. Out through that door.

They all look at her.

Because I think that when we came here, Howard, Daniel and I — and Terry, too, p'raps — we were in a room. And it was quite a pleasant room, we could have stayed for years, quite happily. And that was good, because the door, the only door, in fact, had clicked shut, quietly, behind us . . . But you see, what I think we may have found, the four of us, is that there might be — might just be another door, a different door from the one we came in by, the sort of door we'd never think of, even masquerading as a window or a curtain or a picture on the wall . . . And I think we might have found the strength, and perspicuity, to find that door, that secret door, and open it, and go beyond our cosy room, to something new. (*Pause.*) And of course it may be that it all goes wrong, and even if it doesn't, memories will fade, and it may look as if things have gone back to the way they were before . . . But I think that once we've found the new door, once the old paint's cracked, the locks turned and the hinges loosened, then we'll always know it's there. And even if *we* never open it again, we'll pass it on.

CRESSIDA *is face to face with* HOWARD. *The phone starts to ring.*

Good. Go.

After a moment, HOWARD *shrugs and goes out.* CRESSIDA, DANIEL *and* TERRY *are still. The phone stops.* ALUN *picks up one suitcase,* FRANKIE *the other. But he can't go. He puts down the suitcase.*

ALUN. You know, at Heysham, we didn't get much change, from the power workers, if the truth be told. Bit disappointing really. But where we did get help was from this kind of group who turned up, from the anti-nuclear. Bit freaky actually. Not sure we liked the look of 'em, when they first showed. Not quite sure, to be honest, they was that hygenic. But I have to tell you, that up against our 'brothers' from the power station, going into work, and catcalling, and throwing pennies, all that stuff — well, up against all that, they came up trumps. They stood their ground. And in a day or two, the powermen stopped catcalling, and started looking pretty sheepish, if I'm honest. As they hurried past. And I mean, I can't agree with all they said, but they did all right. Our gypsies. (*Pause.*) 'And it shall come to pass, that all they that look upon thee shall flee from thee, and say, Nineveh is laid waste: who will bemoan her? Whence shall I seek comforters for thee?'

A moment. Then ALUN *goes to* TERRY.

So long, our Terry.

Very gently, he presses his fist against TERRY's *shoulder.* TERRY *responds. Then* ALUN *turns, picks up the suitcase and goes out, followed by* FRANKIE, MICHELE *and* DANIEL.

TERRY. Love it and want to leave it? That's so strange? Is that unprecedented?

CRESSIDA *shakes her head. Enter* HOWARD. TERRY *goes out to the kitchen.*

CRESSIDA. Who was that?

HOWARD. It was for you. He'll ring you back.

CRESSIDA *looks questioning.*

He wouldn't give his name.

CRESSIDA. That's odd.

HOWARD. But I think, in fact, he might be — or he might describe himself — as the bearer of the five-per-cent solution.

CRESSIDA. What.

HOWARD. Or put another way, I have an inkling that, in the hexagram Kuei Mei, where in the sixth place there's an Old Yin line, once again the oracle is wrong.

He walks towards the terrace. As he reaches the windows, he looks around them.

Good heavens. Funny door.

He mimes opening an imaginary door, walks through it to the terrace, and away. CRESSIDA *is looking mystified. Then, suddenly, she rushes round, searching for the 'I Ching'.* DANIEL *re-enters.*

CRESSIDA. Where is it? Where's the *'I Ching'*?

DANIEL. Left it on the terrace.

CRESSIDA. Terrace.

CRESSIDA *goes on to the terrace.* DANIEL *goes out. She finds the book. She reads the section* HOWARD *quoted. She is mystified.*

(*Calls:*) Terry! I think . . . I think in fact, I might be . . . That in fact, you see . . .

She goes out after HOWARD. *The lights change. It's darker, colder.* TERRY *enters with breakfast things. He wears a sweater. He puts down the tray and goes and looks at the weather.*

TERRY. I see.

HOWARD (*calls, from off*). So what's it like?

TERRY (*calls back*). What's what like?

Enter HOWARD *with more breakfast things to put on the table. Like* TERRY, *he is dressed for cooler weather.*

HOWARD. Well, the outlook, comrade.

TERY. Pretty dire.

HOWARD. 'The slightest puff of cloud . . .'

TERRY. Ah me.

They sit at the table for breakfast.

HOWARD. So, do you hear from them?

TERRY. Yes, sure. Don't you?

HOWARD. Well, yes. I mean, from time to time.

TERRY. It's been a year. It's bound −

HOWARD. It's sometimes hard to know, what's best to say.

TERRY. They were betrayed. They were let down.

HOWARD. You think, it's that −

TERRY. Oh, yes. Oh, yes.

Slight pause.

And can *any* of us say, we did enough?

CRESSIDA *enters. She wears the kimono she wore at the beginning of the play. She has a plate of Spanish eggs.*

CRESSIDA. I have made eggs.

She brings the eggs to the table and puts them down.

Yes, I, who could not organise a piss-up on a whelkstall; I, who have misunderstood the situation once again and turned up as a teepee; I, the Married Maiden, whose basket was so unexpectedly not empty after all, I have made eggs. Today. This time. This summer.

A baby has begun to cry. HOWARD *looks up to* CRESSIDA.

HOWARD. Shall I go?

CRESSIDA. Yes. Yes. Why not. You go.

Fade to blackout.